1 CORINTHIANS

Daily Scriptures to Receive,
Reflect, and Respond

DR. HAROLD J. BERRY

Originally published as *1 Corinthians* by Back to the Bible © 2020.

Copyright © 2025 by Dr. Harold J. Berry

Unless otherwise identified, all Scripture quotations in this publication are taken from the Holy Bible, New Living Translation, copyright © 1996, 2004, 2015 by Tyndale House Foundation. Used by permission of Tyndale House Publishers, Inc., Carol Stream, Illinois 60188. All rights reserved.

Cover & Interior Design: © Nelly Murariu at PixBeeDesign.com

ISBN (Paperback): 979-8-9988867-0-6

ISBN (eBook): 979-8-9988867-1-3

Dedication

To My Dear McDonald's Family

For several years now, I've made it my practice to visit McDonald's not just for coffee, but to build genuine friendships. What started as a simple desire to share God's love has blossomed into something far more precious than I ever imagined.

At our particular McDonald's here in Lincoln, Nebraska, what began as casual morning conversations has grown into a circle of friends who have become family to me. We've shared stories, laughter, concerns, and prayers. I've had the privilege of witnessing their kindness, their struggles, and their joys. Together, we've created a little sanctuary of fellowship amid the bustle of breakfast rush.

Then came that unforgettable morning when my world literally turned upside down. One moment I was thinking, "I'm glad I'm sitting down" as dizziness overtook me—and the next thing I knew, I was waking up on the floor, surrounded by the most beautiful faces of concern and care.

In those frightening moments, you became the hands and feet of Christ. One dear friend caught me as I was sliding off my chair, gently guiding me to the floor. Another cradled my head with such tenderness. Someone else immediately called for help while the entire restaurant buzzed with worry for this regular customer who had become so much more than that to all of you.

What moves me most is learning that after the ambulance took me away, you gathered in prayer on my behalf. Even in my absence, your love followed me to the hospital, where—praise God—every test came back normal.

When I walked through those familiar doors a few days later, the relief and joy on your faces told me everything I needed to know about the depth of our friendship. I had always thought of you as fun-loving and kind, but that day revealed something deeper: you are truly precious souls who embody the very love of Christ I had hoped to share with you.

It turns out you were sharing it with me all along.

With profound gratitude and love, I dedicate this study of 1 Corinthians to each of you—my McDonald's family. You have shown me what it means to "bear one another's burdens" and to love not just in word, but in deed and truth.

Your friend always,
Harold J. Berry

CONTENTS

Foreword

We are living in an ever-increasingly polarized world. Jesus followers not only oppose those who view life through a secular lens but also oppose each other! We need the apostle Paul's first letter to the church in Corinth.

Do we need help? Yes! Can 1 Corinthians help us? Indeed, it can!

In it, we learn how to deal with immorality (in the church and outside the church). In it, we find advice on how to disagree with people but still love people. In it, we find hope in the person of Jesus Christ!

Harold Berry opens up 1 Corinthians in a way that all of us can understand and apply. I have known Harold as a family friend, my college Greek professor, a fellow board member at Back to the Bible (Lincoln, NE), and a mentor. A fellow graduate of Dallas Theological Seminary, Harold understands the importance of the Book. He has dedicated his life to teaching the Word. He models what it means to "Teach Truth. Love Well." Before you start reading this volume, read through 1 Corinthians in one sitting. Pray as you read. Ask the Lord to teach you as you read it. Then start going back through it in bite-sized sections and use this volume to help open these truths that we so desperately need to hear today!

Steve Benton
Senior Pastor, Faith Bible Church, Cedar Rapids, Iowa

Week 1:
1 Corinthians 1

RECEIVE

1 Corinthians 1:1

[1] This letter is from Paul, chosen by the will of God to be an apostle of Christ Jesus, and from our brother Sosthenes.

Paul would have some stern things to say in his letter. He wanted the recipients to know that he had been chosen by God, not by men, to be an apostle. It is not certain which Sosthenes it was to whom Paul referred. He may have been the one mentioned in Acts 18:17, or it may have been one by that name copying what Paul was dictating in his letter to the Corinthians.

REFLECT

Do you understand that there were many names that were common names in Bible times even as there are today? This was especially true of the name "Mary."

RESPOND

Join with a friend and read Acts 9:1-19 about Paul's conversion when he was on the road to Damascus. He was chosen by God to be an apostle but did not have the credentials to be chosen as one of the 12 (see Acts 1:21-22).

DAY 2

RECEIVE

1 Corinthians 1:2–3

² I am writing to God's church in Corinth, to you who have been called by God to be his own holy people. He made you holy by means of Christ Jesus, just as he did for all people everywhere who call on the name of our Lord Jesus Christ, their Lord and ours. ³ May God our Father and the Lord Jesus Christ give you grace and peace.

Paul reminded the people in the church in Corinth that they had been called to be God's own holy people. The word "holy" is similar to the one for "sanctified." As such they were also called "saints." He explained how they were made holy. It was the result of them calling on the Lord Jesus Christ. Paul also gave them a greeting that included both grace and peace. Salvation comes by grace through faith in Jesus and the result is peace with God (see Romans 5:1).

REFLECT

Do you realize God also considers you holy if you have trusted in Jesus as Savior?

RESPOND

The word "holy" refers to one who is "set apart." Although the believer's position is that he or she is holy at the time of salvation, by their practice they become more set apart through the Scriptures. See John 17:16–17 for what Jesus said about this.

RECEIVE

DAY 3

1 Corinthians 1:4-6

[4] I always thank my God for you and for the gracious gifts he has given you, now that you belong to Christ Jesus. [5] Through him, God has enriched your church in every way—with all of your eloquent words and all of your knowledge. [6] This confirms that what I told you about Christ is true.

It is interesting to notice in a letter's introduction how items are mentioned that are later referred to in the letter. Paul will have much to write the Corinthians about gifts and speaking in tongues. Here verse 5 seems to be a reference to those matters. God had enriched their church in many ways, but it will be seen that the Corinthian church had many problems.

REFLECT

Do you realize that, as a believer, God has enriched your life, but it does not mean you are without problems?

RESPOND

With a friend talk about the importance of having harmony in the church fellowship. Read John 13:35 for what Jesus said about how to show the world that believers are really His disciples.

RECEIVE

1 Corinthians 1:7–9

[7] Now you have every spiritual gift you need as you eagerly wait for the return of our Lord Jesus Christ. [8] He will keep you strong to the end so that you will be free from all blame on the day when our Lord Jesus Christ returns. [9] God will do this, for he is faithful to do what he says, and he has invited you into partnership with his Son, Jesus Christ our Lord.

1 Corinthians 12 will discuss spiritual gifts, and here Paul tells the believers in the church that they have every spiritual gift they need. Above all Paul wanted them to be without blame on the day Jesus returns. No one is perfect, but to be without blame would at least mean when one does wrong he or she will admit it and endeavor to make it right with the wronged person.

REFLECT

As a believer, think about how blessed you are to be a partner with God's Son, the Lord Jesus Christ. Because of this, you should forgive others as He has forgiven you.

RESPOND

To see that Paul will answer questions about spiritual gifts, read 1 Corinthians 12:1–3. He will have much to say in that chapter.

DAY 5

RECEIVE

1 Corinthians 1:10

[10] I appeal to you, dear brothers and sisters, by the authority of our Lord Jesus Christ, to live in harmony with each other. Let there be no divisions in the church. Rather, be of one mind, united in thought and purpose.

Paul wanted believers to live in harmony with each other. He did not want there to be any divisions in the church. He did not mean they all had to think alike, but they needed to have the same goals in mind. Some churches lack a distinctive purpose; that would not have pleased the apostle Paul.

REFLECT

Even though there are differences of opinion in your church, do the people have the same goals in mind?

RESPOND

With a friend read Philippians 2:1-8 about what Paul wrote the Philippian believers about using Christ as their example. Especially notice what Jesus' attitude was.

WEEK 2:
1 CORINTHIANS 1

DAY 1

1 Corinthians 1:11-12

[11] For some members of Chloe's household have told me about your quarrels, my dear brothers and sisters. [12] Some of you are saying, "I am a follower of Paul." Others are saying, "I follow Apollos," or "I follow Peter," or "I follow only Christ."

Paul had appealed for the believers in Corinth to have harmony with no divisions. These verses tell what he had heard about their fellowship. They had become divided about which leader they wished to follow. The fourth group he mentioned put themselves up as the most spiritual by saying, "I follow only Christ."

REFLECT

Are there divisions in your church assembly over who has been your best pastor? If so, you are experiencing what the Corinthian church was experiencing. That which is most important is the Word of God that was proclaimed; not who the messenger is or was.

RESPOND

With a friend read about the works of the flesh in Galatians 5:19-21. Notice that "division" is one mentioned. This does not seem to be the full list because Paul added "and other sins like these." Read also Proverbs 6:16-19 about seven things the Lord hates. Especially notice the last one.

DAY 2

RECEIVE

1 Corinthians 1:13-15

[13] Has Christ been divided into factions? Was I, Paul, crucified for you? Were any of you baptized in the name of Paul? Of course not! [14] I thank God that I did not baptize any of you except Crispus and Gaius, [15] for now no one can say they were baptized in my name.

Notice that Paul used himself as an example in refuting what the Corinthian believers were saying. Paul let it be known he was not the one who was crucified for them. Also, baptism is an issue with many people and some are proud of the one who baptized them. Paul was glad he had rarely baptized anyone so people could not say they were baptized by him.

REFLECT

Do you know of people who take pride about the person who baptized them?

RESPOND

Talk with a friend about what is most important—the person who baptized you or the significance of why you were baptized.

RECEIVE

DAY 3

1 Corinthians 1:16-17

¹⁶ (Oh yes, I also baptized the household of Stephanas, but I don't remember baptizing anyone else.) ¹⁷ For Christ didn't send me to baptize, but to preach the Good News—and not with clever speech, for fear that the cross of Christ would lose its power.

Having mentioned that he had baptized Crispus and Gaius, Paul then remembered he had baptized the household of Stephanas. He points out, however, that his main mission was not to baptize but to preach the gospel. He emphasized how he had preached—"not with clever speech." Paul did not want anything to detract from the message of the cross of Christ.

REFLECT

Does this help you see that although baptism is important, it is not as important as the message of salvation itself? The thief on the cross was not baptized, but he believed in Jesus to save him.

RESPOND

With a friend read John 4:1-2. This passage reveals that Jesus left the baptizing to his disciples. His primary concern was helping people see how to become right with God. Once they expressed faith, they could show through baptism that they were identifying with Jesus and His followers.

RECEIVE

1 Corinthians 1:18-19

[18] The message of the cross is foolish to those who are headed for destruction! But we who are being saved know it is the very power of God. [19] As the Scriptures say, "I will destroy the wisdom of the wise and discard the intelligence of the intelligent."

Paul expressed how the message of the cross was considered by others. It seemed as foolishness to unbelievers. To those who believed and were on the path to salvation, it was the power of God. Paul referred to the Old Testament Scriptures when he cited Isaiah 29:14.

REFLECT

As you read the Old Testament Scriptures, do you see parallels with what is said in the Old Testament? Jesus referred to this connection often, such as in Matthew 24:15, 37-39.

RESPOND

Paul referred to those "who are being saved." Salvation is sometimes looked at in three aspects: justification (believing in Jesus); sanctification (being set apart by His Word); and glorification (when the person goes to be with Jesus at death).

RECEIVE

1 Corinthians 1:20-21

[20] So where does this leave the philosophers, the scholars, and the world's brilliant debaters? God has made the wisdom of this world look foolish. [21] Since God in his wisdom saw to it that the world would never know him through human wisdom, he has used our foolish preaching to save those who believe.

Paul revealed that spiritual matters do not depend on one having a brilliant mind. People do not come to God by human wisdom; it is by believing the simple word that is preached about the cross. In so doing, God has made the wisdom of the world look foolish. One should not apologize for not being brilliant; the most important matter is to believe in the Lord Jesus Christ.

REFLECT

Rather than thinking about how intelligent you are, think rather about the salvation you have in Jesus by trusting Him as Savior. This is your greatest gift.

RESPOND

With a friend read the introduction in the book of Proverbs. Especially notice 1:1-7 that tells what the various proverbs will produce in a person. There are 31 chapters in Proverbs. Some have made a habit of reading the chapter in Proverbs that matches the day of the month.

WEEK 3:
1 CORINTHIANS 1

RECEIVE

1 Corinthians 1:22-23

²² It is foolish to the Jews, who ask for signs from heaven. And it is foolish to the Greeks, who seek human wisdom. ²³ So when we preach that Christ was crucified, the Jews are offended and the Gentiles say it's all nonsense.

Paul revealed what the gospel of the Lord Jesus Christ appeared like to various groups. The Jewish people who were always looking for a sign; Paul said the gospel to them was like something they stumbled over and they were offended. The Greeks who sought human wisdom; the gospel to them seemed as nonsense.

REFLECT

Have you had some sneer at the gospel message? Do they think it is too simple that one could have forgiveness of sin and eternal life by believing in Jesus? If so, they don't believe what the Word of God teaches, and that is the only book God has inspired.

RESPOND

With a friend read passages that clearly point out how one becomes right with God. See John 3:16-18; 14:6; Acts 4:12; Romans 5:1; Ephesians 2:8-9. Talk about how to use these verses when witnessing to others.

DAY 2

RECEIVE

1 Corinthians 1:24-25

²⁴ But to those called by God to salvation, both Jews and Gentiles, Christ is the power of God and the wisdom of God. ²⁵ This foolish plan of God is wiser than the wisest of human plans, and God's weakness is stronger than the greatest of human strength.

The gospel seems as foolishness to some. But for those of all nationalities who are called by God, they realize the gospel is "the power of God and the wisdom of God." The result is that what to human reasoning seems to be foolishness is wiser than the wisest of human plans. Jewish thinking was one of contrasts. Paul explained that "God's weakness is stronger than the greatest of human strength."

REFLECT

Do you realize that salvation in Jesus by believing in His death on the cross for you is far greater than any human reasoning could devise?

RESPOND

Join with a friend in seeing verses that show contrast in Jewish thinking. Luke 14:26 has confused many about hating parents. One's love for parents should seem like hate in contrast to how much one loves God. Romans 9:13 is a contrast of Jacob and Esau. Both were given promises of God, but Jacob's were so much greater it seemed as if Esau's were hate by comparison.

DAY 3

RECEIVE

1 Corinthians 1:26-27

[26] Remember, dear brothers and sisters, that few of you were wise in the world's eyes or powerful or wealthy when God called you. [27] Instead, God chose things the world considers foolish in order to shame those who think they are wise. And he chose things that are powerless to shame those who are powerful.

Paul told of how the world's values, no matter how high, could not compare to what God has done. One's wealth does not make the person any closer to God than one's poverty. Some have much education in the world with degrees after their names. Before God, that does not make them wiser than the uneducated who have faith in God.

REFLECT

Have you felt intimidated before some who are highly educated? You need not. If you have trusted in Jesus as Savior you have more spiritual wisdom than the educated who are unsaved.

RESPOND

Consider with a friend the statement in Proverbs 1:7. It shows what true wisdom is. Consider also James 1:5. Talk about how important it is to know the wisdom of God.

DAY 4

RECEIVE

1 Corinthians 1:28-29

[28] God chose things despised by the world, things counted as nothing at all, and used them to bring to nothing what the world considers important. [29] As a result, no one can ever boast in the presence of God.

Paul continued to show the importance of those whom God uses. He sometimes chooses those the world considers the least likely to succeed to be spiritual giants and turn many to faith in Jesus. It seems to delight God to choose what the world considers important to show how unimportant it is. It also delights Him to choose a humble sinner who trusts in Him to be of greater use than one the world would vote for.

REFLECT

Does this help you to think more about what you have spiritually than what you have physically?

RESPOND

Believers in Jesus have nothing to boast about. All they can do is thank the Lord for choosing and using them for His glory.

DAY 5

RECEIVE

1 Corinthians 1:30–31

³⁰ God has united you with Christ Jesus. For our benefit God made him to be wisdom itself. Christ made us right with God; he made us pure and holy, and he freed us from sin. ³¹ Therefore, as the Scriptures say, "If you want to boast, boast only about the Lord."

What the believer has is because of what God has done for him or her. Paul cited the heart of Jeremiah 9:24 when he told all believers, "If you want to boast, boast only about the Lord." 1 Corinthians 1:30 tells that God the Father made the Son to be "wisdom itself." The Father and the Son have done so many things for the believer in Jesus.

REFLECT

Think on 1 Corinthians 1:30 and what it says the Father and the Son have done for believers. If you have trusted in Jesus, you are included in this group.

RESPOND

With a friend read 1 Peter 1:3-7 to see what Peter was telling those being persecuted and scattered because of their faith. Jesus is all the believer needs. Read the longer verse in Jeremiah 9:24 to see how Paul only gave the main point of it.

WEEK 4:
1 CORINTHIANS 2

RECEIVE

1 Corinthians 2:1-2

[1] When I first came to you, dear brothers and sisters, I didn't use lofty words and impressive wisdom to tell you God's secret plan. [2] For I decided that while I was with you I would forget everything except Jesus Christ, the one who was crucified.

Notice how Paul kept the main thing the main thing. He did not try to impress with his vocabulary and personality. His main message was about Jesus Christ who had been crucified not only for the world but also for the Corinthians to whom Paul was writing. Nothing was more important to Paul than talking about the crucifixion of Jesus.

REFLECT

Does this help you to understand how to be more effective in your Christian witness?

RESPOND

With a friend read Romans 6:5-7 to see how the believer participates in the death and resurrection of Jesus. Visit with each other about what Jesus has accomplished for each of you.

DAY 2

RECEIVE

1 Corinthians 2:3-5

³ I came to you in weakness—timid and trembling. ⁴ And my message and my preaching were very plain. Rather than using clever and persuasive speeches, I relied only on the power of the Holy Spirit. ⁵ I did this so you would trust not in human wisdom but in the power of God.

It is easy to think the apostles were so strong in their faith they had no fears in sharing the gospel. Corinth was a corrupt place at this time—morally, religiously, and economically. It was what one might call a "den of iniquity." Paul did not seek to win anyone with his personality and wisdom; he wanted them to trust in the power of God.

REFLECT

As you think of the one who led you to place your trust in Jesus, was it the personality of the individual or the message the person presented?

RESPOND

Paul relied only on the "power of the Holy Spirit." With a friend look at other passages that mention this same expression. See Romans 1:3-4; 2 Timothy 1:13-14; 1 Peter 1:10-12; Jude 1:19-21.

DAY 3

RECEIVE

1 Corinthians 2:6-7

⁶ Yet when I am among mature believers, I do speak with words of wisdom, but not the kind of wisdom that belongs to this world or to the rulers of this world, who are soon forgotten. ⁷ No, the wisdom we speak of is the mystery of God—his plan that was previously hidden, even though he made it for our ultimate glory before the world began.

Paul contrasted human wisdom with spiritual wisdom. He referred to a "mystery," which in the Bible refers to something previously unknown but is then being made known. God's plan had been hidden from the beginning but would now be revealed.

REFLECT

Do you realize that the New Testament Church is never referred to in the Old Testament? Israel is the focus there, not the body of Christ known as the Church.

RESPOND

With a friend examine some passages that have to do with mysteries revealed in the New Testament. See Romans 11:24-26; Ephesians 3:1-6; 5:31-33; 1 Timothy 3:16. These verses reveal some of the plans God had that are revealed in the New Testament but were not in the Old Testament.

DAY 4

RECEIVE

1 Corinthians 2:8-9

⁸ But the rulers of this world have not understood it; if they had, they would not have crucified our glorious Lord. ⁹ That is what the Scriptures mean when they say, "No eye has seen, no ear has heard, and no mind has imagined what God has prepared for those who love him."

Some use this verse out of context. On the one hand it seems to refer to things one could never dream about. On the other hand, the explanation comes in the following verses. Those verses will explain what "God has prepared for those who love him." This is another occasion when a question that might arise from one verse or verses is answered later on.

REFLECT

Have you learned to keep reading when you have questions about what the Bible says?

RESPOND

With a friend read some verses in Revelation that make one wonder about the meaning but are explained later. See an example in Revelation 1:11-12 about the "seven gold lampstands." Then read Revelation 1:20 that explains what they are.

DAY 5

RECEIVE

1 Corinthians 2:10-11

¹⁰ But it was to us that God revealed these things by his Spirit. For his Spirit searches out everything and shows us God's deep secrets. ¹¹ No one can know a person's thoughts except that person's own spirit and no one can know God's thoughts except God's own Spirit.

1 Corinthians 2:9 said "No eye has seen, no ear has heard, and no mind has imagined what God has prepared for those who love him." Verse 10 reveals what God has revealed by His Spirit. The way one human can understand what another human's thoughts are is because each has the same human spirit in them. To know God's thoughts, one must have the same divine Spirit. This refers to the Holy Spirit.

REFLECT

Does this help you understand why the Scriptures became more understandable to you once you trusted Jesus as Savior and received the Holy Spirit?

RESPOND

Join with another and read 2 Corinthians 4:3-4. This passage helps one to understand why an unbeliever thinks the gospel is foolishness and it seems hidden to him.

WEEK 5:
1 CORINTHIANS 2, 3

RECEIVE

DAY 1

1 Corinthians 2:12

[12] And we have received God's Spirit (not the world's spirit), so we can know the wonderful things God has freely given us.

How can one know the things of God? Just as one human understands another human because they have the same spirit, people can know the things of God by receiving His Holy Spirit, the third person of the Trinity. Then the individual has the same spirit so he or she "can know the wonderful things God has freely given us." One of the important truths of living the Christian life is to understand that at salvation you received the Holy Spirit who took up residence in your inner person.

REFLECT

Have you been taught that you received the indwelling Holy Spirit when you trusted Jesus as Savior? This is an extremely important teaching.

RESPOND

Join with a friend to examine some Scriptures about receiving the Holy Spirit. Examine passages such as John 14:16-17, 26; Romans 8:9; 1 Corinthians 6:19; 12:12-13. This is teaching that is based on these and other Scriptures.

DAY 2

RECEIVE

1 Corinthians 2:13-14

¹³ When we tell you these things, we do not use words that come from human wisdom. Instead, we speak words given to us by the Spirit, using the Spirit's words to explain spiritual truths. ¹⁴ But people who aren't spiritual can't receive these truths from God's Spirit. It all sounds foolish to them and they can't understand it, for only those who are spiritual can understand what the Spirit means.

Paul continued to explain the difference between the saved and the unsaved. He explained why those not born again by trusting in Jesus are unable to understand spiritual truths. Those not born again only understand human wisdom. Those born again have the indwelling Holy Spirit and can understand spiritual truths.

REFLECT

Does this help you better understand why in the same group of people there are some who seem to understand spiritual truths and those who do not?

RESPOND

Talk with a friend about the difference of the natural person and the spiritual one. The natural one is the one who has had the birth on earth but has not had the birth that comes from God above and is considered to be born again. The believer has God's Spirit in him to help him understand the truths of God.

DAY 3

RECEIVE

1 Corinthians 2:15-16

¹⁵ Those who are spiritual can evaluate all things, but they themselves cannot be evaluated by others. ¹⁶ For, "Who can know the Lord's thoughts? Who knows enough to teach him?" But we understand these things, for we have the mind of Christ.

This does not mean the believer knows everything, but he or she has the capacity to evaluate the things of God. This verse also indicates others do not understand the spiritual person. The followers of Jesus have "the mind of Christ" so they are spiritually equipped to understand the truths of God.

REFLECT

If you are a follower of Jesus, does this help you understand why those who are not Christ followers sometimes do not understand you? You are thinking about eternal matters; they think only of earthly concerns.

RESPOND

Visit with a friend about a veil seeming to be over the faces of those who are not Christ followers. Read 2 Corinthians 3:16-18 to help your thinking in this regard.

RECEIVE

1 Corinthians 3:1–2

[1] Dear brothers and sisters, when I was with you I couldn't talk to you as I would to spiritual people. I had to talk as though you belonged to this world or as though you were infants in Christ. [2] I had to feed you with milk, not with solid food, because you weren't ready for anything stronger. And you still aren't ready . . .

Paul had contrasted the natural with the spiritual. Then he presents another category of people. They are believers because he referred to them as "infants in Christ." He had to treat them as new believers instead of ones who by this time should have been mature believers. He had to talk to them as though they belonged to the world. They are commonly referred to as "carnal" because they were living according to the flesh rather than according to the Spirit.

REFLECT

How is it with you? Have you progressed in the Christian faith to the extent you are able to evaluate the things of God and not just the elementary truths of the Scripture?

RESPOND

Paul referred the immature Christians as ones who needed to be fed with milk instead of solid food. To see how one progresses from the milk stage to the meat stage, join with a friend in reading Hebrews 5:11–14. As one is in the Word of God that individual becomes more spiritually mature and better at distinguishing right from wrong.

DAY 5

RECEIVE

1 Corinthians 3:3-4

³ . . . for you are still controlled by your sinful nature. You are jealous of one another and quarrel with each other. Doesn't that prove you are controlled by your sinful nature? Aren't you living like people of the world? ⁴ When one of you says, "I am a follower of Paul," and another says, "I follow Apollos," aren't you acting just like people of the world?

Paul had some strong words for these Christians living according to the flesh. How did he know this? It was because he had been told how they were divided over messengers of God rather than the message of God. This divisive spirit revealed to him they were "acting just like people of the world." They were jealous and quarreling with each other over these matters.

REFLECT

How is it in your church assembly? Are people divided over who is the better teacher rather than being more concerned about the teaching itself?

RESPOND

Talk with a friend about how a local assembly of believers can reveal to the watching world that they are true believers. See what Jesus said in John 13:34-35. Is this evident in your local church?

WEEK 6:
1 CORINTHIANS 3

RECEIVE

1 Corinthians 3:5-6

⁵ After all, who is Apollos? Who is Paul? We are only God's servants through whom you believed the Good News. Each of us did the work the Lord gave us. ⁶ I planted the seed in your hearts, and Apollos watered it, but it was God who made it grow.

The Corinthian believers had been arguing about the best speaker and teacher. Some thought Apollos; others thought Paul. Here Paul emphasizes both of them are only the messengers of God doing what the Lord gave them to do. Paul had given the gospel message; Apollos had watered it; but it was "God who made it grow."

REFLECT

Are you aware in your witnessing for Jesus that you can only tell others about Him; only God can convert the heart?

RESPOND

Talk about these verses with a friend from your local church. Be thankful for others who have planted the spiritual seed and for others who had watered it. Be especially thankful to God who changed hearts as they believed in Him. Talk also about which part each of you can have in the sowing and watering ministries.

RECEIVE

1 Corinthians 3:7-9

[7] It's not important who does the planting, or who does the watering. What's important is that God makes the seed grow. [8] The one who plants and the one who waters work together with the same purpose. And both will be rewarded for their own hard work. [9] For we are both God's workers. And you are God's field. You are God's building.

Paul minimized the part he and Apollos had in God's work. He and Apollos had worked together with the same purpose in mind. As they were faithful in doing what God wanted them to do, each could expect to be rewarded. In verse 9, Paul changes the metaphor from God's field to God's building. He will focus on the building in the following verses.

REFLECT

As you talk to others about Jesus, you may be planting the seed for the first time or watering what someone else planted before you. Thank God for the part each of you have.

RESPOND

As you pray for others, consider what Paul prayed for the ones he loved. Read Ephesians 3:14-19 to see one of Paul's prayers for others. You and a friend should discuss this prayer and how it can relate to your own prayer lives.

DAY 3

RECEIVE

1 Corinthians 3:10-11

[10] Because of God's grace to me, I have laid the foundation like an expert builder. Now others are building on it. But whoever is building on this foundation must be very careful. [11] For no one can lay any foundation other than the one we already have—Jesus Christ.

Having mentioned God's building in verse 9, Paul proceeded to use that example for some spiritual truths. He had laid the spiritual foundation in the lives of individuals. Others built on that foundation. There is only one true foundation; that is Jesus Christ Himself. By telling others the gospel message, Paul had laid this foundation in their lives.

REFLECT

Which part do you think God has given you? Are you one who has the privilege of giving the gospel message and laying the foundation; or are you one who builds on what others have done? Both are important and God uses both kinds.

RESPOND

Notice the warning not to try to build a spiritual foundation other than the Lord Jesus Christ. With a friend, read Galatians 1:6-9 to see what Paul said about anyone who preached a different gospel than what he was preaching.

RECEIVE

DAY 4

1 Corinthians 3:12-13

¹² Anyone who builds on that foundation may use a variety of materials—gold, silver, jewels, wood, hay, or straw. ¹³ But on the judgment day, fire will reveal what kind of work each builder has done. The fire will show if a person's work has any value.

Notice the subject in these verses. It is not the one who laid the foundation; it is the one who builds on it. The "judgment day" referred to is also known as the *Bēma* or "judgment seat of God" (see Romans 14:10). If you are teaching believers, you are building on the foundation someone else has laid. In the analogy, the gold, silver, jewels, wood, hay, or straw are symbolic and not strewn around heaven. It is logical to conclude that the fire is symbolic also and not actual. These have to do with quality, not quantity, of one's spiritual work.

REFLECT

Let this Bible passage be a reminder of doing Christian work with the right motives.

RESPOND

Talk with a believer about the difference of the quality of one's ministry in contrast to the quantity of it. Verse 13 in the study refers to whether the work has value. Some translations render it "of what sort it is."

RECEIVE

1 Corinthians 3:14-15

¹⁴ If the work survives, that builder will receive a reward.
¹⁵ But if the work is burned up, the builder will suffer great loss.
The builder will be saved, but like someone barely escaping
through a wall of flames.

This passage reveals the results of testing the quality of the believer's works. When there is quality there will be a reward. When there is no quality, the loss suffered will be the loss of rewards. Salvation is not in question. All who stand before this judgment are believers in Jesus.

REFLECT

Knowing that you do not lose salvation once you've put your trust in Jesus should cause you to want to live to please Him in all you do.

RESPOND

Talk with a friend about distinguishing between salvation and rewards. Salvation is secure for all who believe in Jesus; rewards depend on how the believer serves Him.

WEEK 7:
1 CORINTHIANS 3, 4

RECEIVE

1 Corinthians 3:16–17

¹⁶ Don't you realize that all of you together are the temple of God and that the Spirit of God lives in you? ¹⁷ God will destroy anyone who destroys this temple. For God's temple is holy, and you are that temple.

Although each believer in Jesus is considered to be a temple of the Holy Spirit, Paul seems to be referring here to the collective group in the local church. This is because the "you" is plural in the Greek text. The local church that is made up of those who are Christ followers is also seen as God's temple. It would be serious for anyone with false teaching to seek to destroy it.

REFLECT

As a believer in Jesus, do you realize that the Holy Spirit lives in you as well as in other believers?

RESPOND

Join with another believer and read 1 Corinthians 6:15–20. This passage reveals that even though the Holy Spirit is everywhere present, He also resides in the inner person of every believer in Jesus.

DAY 2

RECEIVE

1 Corinthians 3:18-20

[18] Stop deceiving yourselves. If you think you are wise by this world's standards, you need to become a fool to be truly wise. [19] For the wisdom of this world is foolishness to God. As the Scriptures say, "He traps the wise in the snare of their own cleverness." [20] And again, "The Lord knows the thoughts of the wise; he knows they are worthless."

No matter how wise a person is with this world's wisdom, that wisdom is considered as foolishness in comparison to God's wisdom. In verse 19 Paul cites Job 5:13. In verse 20 he cites Psalm 94:11. Paul was thoroughly acquainted with the Hebrew Scriptures and often drew parallels to them.

REFLECT

When a cross reference is given in your copy of the Scriptures, do you take time to look it up? It is a good way to do Bible study.

RESPOND

Apparently those in the Corinthian church were being impressed with some teachers who seemed to be wise but were not teaching the true gospel. Paul did not want those believers to have their confidence in those who only pleased their hearing. See 2 Timothy 4:1-4 in this regard.

RECEIVE

DAY 3

1 Corinthians 3:21-23

[21] So don't boast about following a particular human leader. For everything belongs to you— [22] whether Paul or Apollos or Peter, or the world, or life and death, or the present and the future. Everything belongs to you, [23] and you belong to Christ, and Christ belongs to God.

Paul reminded them of the debate they were having about who was the best human leader. He had chided them over this in 1 Corinthians 3:3-4. As he returned to this issue he mentioned himself first as he listed "whether Paul or Apollos or Peter." Paul did not want them being followers of him or others. He wanted the Corinthian believers to realize they had all they needed in Jesus.

REFLECT

Do you realize that God has given you a divine teacher because He has given every believer the Holy Spirit?

RESPOND

Join with a friend in seeing some Bible references to the teaching of the Holy Spirit. Examine passages such as John 14:26; 15:26; 1 Timothy 4:1.

RECEIVE

1 Corinthians 4:1–2

[1]So look at Apollos and me as mere servants of Christ who have been put in charge of explaining God's mysteries. [2] Now, a person who is put in charge as a manager must be faithful.

Apparently some in the Corinthian church were especially impressed with Apollos. Perhaps he had a more illustrious oratory than the apostle Paul. The believers needed to be reminded that the most important thing about any servant—as both Apollos and he were— is faithfulness.

REFLECT

Can you always be counted on to do what you say you will do? That is being faithful.

RESPOND

Talk with a friend about the importance of being faithful. Read Luke 16:10 that records what Jesus said about this.

DAY 5

RECEIVE

1 Corinthians 4:3-4

³ As for me, it matters very little how I might be evaluated by you or by any human authority. I don't even trust my own judgment on this point. ⁴ My conscience is clear, but that doesn't prove I'm right. It is the Lord himself who will examine me and decide.

Others were evaluating who had the better ministry among them. Paul did not pay any attention to what they thought nor did he even evaluate his own feelings. He would leave it to the Lord to make the true evaluation.

REFLECT

Although you should not do things with the wrong motive, it is not wise to keep doing introspection. You can spend so much time looking inward you have little time to look outward to others.

RESPOND

Matthew 7:1 says not to judge or you will be judged. Yet verse 7:6 says "Don't waste what is holy on people who are unholy. Don't throw your pearls to pigs! They will trample the pearls, then turn and attack you." This would include making judgments about what falls in the category of pearls and who falls in the category of pigs. Actions can be judged; what cannot be judged are motives. Talk about this with a friend.

WEEK 8:
1 CORINTHIANS 4

RECEIVE

1 Corinthians 4:5

[5] So don't make judgments about anyone ahead of time—before the Lord returns. For he will bring our darkest secrets to light and will reveal our private motives. Then God will give to each one whatever praise is due.

Paul urged believers not to judge people ahead of time. They should leave the judging to God who knows about secret motives and can reward accordingly. This makes the point that although actions can be judged, motives cannot be. It will be evident in 1 Corinthians 5 that Paul wanted them to judge the actions of a person, but he does not refer to his motives.

REFLECT

Does it help you to know you should not judge a person's motives even if the person's actions should be judged?

RESPOND

With a friend read Romans 14:1-10. This passage shows what Paul wrote about not judging someone regarding the person's diet or day of worship. Talk with your friend about following Paul's advice.

RECEIVE

1 Corinthians 4:6-7

[6] Dear brothers and sisters, I have used Apollos and myself to illustrate what I've been saying. If you pay attention to what I have quoted from the Scriptures, you won't be proud of one of your leaders at the expense of another. [7] For what gives you the right to make such a judgment? What do you have that God hasn't given you? And if everything you have is from God, why boast as though it were not a gift?

Paul did not want the Corinthian believers to judge who they thought was the best leader at the expense of another leader. He did not want them to be proud of a particular leader that would put another leader in a bad light. Speakers are gifted by God in different ways. To be critical of leaders, therefore, is to be questioning God.

REFLECT

Do you accept various Bible teachers as those gifted by God with different approaches? The same Word of God is shown through various personalities.

RESPOND

Chapters in the New Testament concerning spiritual gifts can be thought of as two 12s and two 4s. 1 Corinthians 12; Romans 12; Ephesians 4; 1 Peter 4. With a friend, search for the verses in each of these chapters that tell about gifts and gifted people.

RECEIVE

DAY 3

1 Corinthians 4:8-9

[8] You think you already have everything you need. You think you are already rich. You have begun to reign in God's kingdom without us! I wish you really were reigning already, for then we would be reigning with you. [9] Instead, I sometimes think God has put us apostles on display, like prisoners of war at the end of a victor's parade, condemned to die. We have become a spectacle to the entire world—to people and angels alike.

Paul scolded the Corinthian believers who thought glory would come before suffering. He contrasted their thoughts with what the apostles were experiencing. To him, it seemed like the apostles had become a "spectacle to the entire world." He realized that suffering came before glory.

REFLECT

As a believer in Jesus, are you suffering now for your faith? If so, you can count on rewards and glory later.

RESPOND

Read Romans 8:18-25 with a Christian friend. This will encourage both of you as you realize whatever you are experiencing, glory will follow.

RECEIVE

DAY 4

1 Corinthians 4:10-11

¹⁰ Our dedication to Christ makes us look like fools, but you claim to be so wise in Christ! We are weak, but you are so powerful! You are honored, but we are ridiculed. ¹¹ Even now we go hungry and thirsty, and we don't have enough clothes to keep warm. We are often beaten and have no home.

In contrast to what the Corinthian believers seemed to be thinking, Paul thought the dedication of the apostles must make them look foolish. The apostles were experiencing hardships while the believers in Corinth were not experiencing suffering. The contrast seemed extreme.

REFLECT

Are you discouraged as you compare your circumstances with what others seem to be experiencing?

RESPOND

Join with a friend in praying for what some are going through as they seek to serve Jesus. Some live in areas of the world where it could cost their lives if they claim to be His followers.

RECEIVE

DAY 5

1 Corinthians 4:12-13

[12] We work wearily with our own hands to earn our living. We bless those who curse us. We are patient with those who abuse us. [13] We appeal gently when evil things are said about us. Yet we are treated like the world's garbage, like everybody's trash—right up to the present moment.

Paul expressed what the apostles were experiencing. They were working hard to earn their living. Yet, instead of having a bad attitude about others, the apostles were blessing others even while they were being mistreated. Paul said the apostles were being treated "like everybody's trash."

REFLECT

Imagine what Paul and the others felt like as they sought to teach what Jesus taught and lived to honor Him. Have you sometimes felt like this?

RESPOND

Visit with a friend about what Paul said he thought of his present position in Christ in contrast to his previous life. Read Philippians 3:5-11 where Paul wrote about this. There was nothing that would cause Paul to want to give up what he had in knowing Jesus as Savior.

WEEK 9:
1 CORINTHIANS 4, 5

RECEIVE

1 Corinthians 4:14-16

[14] I am not writing these things to shame you, but to warn you as my beloved children. [15] For even if you had ten thousand others to teach you about Christ, you have only one spiritual father. For I became your father in Christ Jesus when I preached the Good News to you. [16] So I urge you to imitate me.

Sometimes younger people in the faith need to be warned of certain things. Paul did this as he wrote to them. He let them know of his special interest in them. He reminded them they may have other teachers telling them about Jesus, but he became their father in Christ when he preached the gospel to them. As a result, he urged them to mimic him.

REFLECT

Have you had a spiritual parent warn you about some things? Did you understand this was for your good?

RESPOND

Do you have a spiritual parent to imitate? Do you live in such a way you can ask others to mimic you? Talk with a friend about this.

RECEIVE

1 Corinthians 4:17
¹⁷ That's why I have sent Timothy, my beloved and faithful child in the Lord. He will remind you of how I follow Christ Jesus, just as I teach in all the churches wherever I go.

Paul had been like a spiritual father to Timothy. He wrote two letters to him that were inspired of God and retained in the Bible: 1 and 2 Timothy. Perhaps Timothy's mother taught him about Jesus and led him to trust in Him (see Acts 16:1-5). As in 1 Corinthians 4:17, Paul considered Timothy his "beloved and faithful child in the Lord." He had been a special mentor to Timothy. Timothy would remind the Corinthians how Paul followed the Lord Jesus everywhere.

REFLECT

Do you have someone who serves as a Paul in your life? Do you have someone who depends on you as a Timothy? Think about this.

RESPOND

Join with a believer and read verses that tell about being imitators of a Christian leader. See 1 Corinthians 11:1; 1 Thessalonians 1:6; 2:14; Hebrews 6:12. If you are imitating Jesus, it will not be difficult to ask others to imitate you.

RECEIVE

DAY 3

1 Corinthians 4:18-19

[18] Some of you have become arrogant, thinking I will not visit you again. [19] But I will come—and soon—if the Lord lets me, and then I'll find out whether these arrogant people just give pretentious speeches or whether they really have God's power.

Paul corrected some for their attitude. They seemed to have a proud attitude toward what was going on in their church fellowship. It was easy to feel that way without Paul being present, but he warned them that he planned to visit them. Paul would then learn how arrogant they would act.

REFLECT

Have you noticed that people will sometimes talk critically about a leader if he is absent? How do they act when he is present?

RESPOND

Join with a friend in reading Ephesians 4:30-32. This passage tells of the need to forgive others as Christ has forgiven you. Talk about this and seek to practice it.

RECEIVE

DAY 4

1 Corinthians 4:20-21

[20] For the Kingdom of God is not just a lot of talk; it is living by God's power. [21] Which do you choose? Should I come with a rod to punish you, or should I come with love and a gentle spirit?

Some can talk boldly, but Paul wanted them to know the Kingdom of God was not made up of just talk. They should be more concerned about "living by God's power." Paul indicated they could choose talk or God's power. Paul also gave them the choice of how they would like to see him when he came to them again.

REFLECT

Have these verses helped you to focus more on living to please Jesus rather than being arrogant and critical of others?

RESPOND

Read Colossians 3:12-17 with a friend. Talk about practicing these principles that the apostle Paul presented.

RECEIVE

DAY 5

1 Corinthians 5:1-2

[1] I can hardly believe the report about the sexual immorality going on among you—something that even pagans don't do. I am told that a man in your church is living in sin with his stepmother. [2] You are so proud of yourselves, but you should be mourning in sorrow and shame. And you should remove this man from your fellowship.

Paul came to a difficult portion in his letter to the Corinthian believers. Something was going on in their local fellowship that they needed to be confronted about. It is considered that his father's wife is actually his stepmother. Rather than the group being ashamed of what was occurring in their midst, they seemed to be proud of their tolerance. Paul made the difficult statement, "You should remove this man from your fellowship."

REFLECT

Have you had situations in your local assembly that someone needed to be expelled from it?

RESPOND

Church discipline is a controversial topic. Some churches seem to be quick to expel members; others seem not to expel anyone no matter how the person is living.

WEEK 10:
1 CORINTHIANS 5

RECEIVE

1 Corinthians 5:3-4

³ Even though I am not with you in person, I am with you in the Spirit. And as though I were there, I have already passed judgment on this man ⁴ in the name of the Lord Jesus. You must call a meeting of the church. I will be present with you in spirit, and so will the power of our Lord Jesus.

Even though he was not with the Corinthian believers, Paul said he was with them in the Spirit. The apostle had already passed judgment on this person who was living in sin with his stepmother. He instructed that a meeting of the church should be called and both he, in spirit, and the "power of the Lord Jesus" would be with them.

REFLECT

Do you agree with the apostle Paul that this sin should have been dealt with by the church?

RESPOND

With a friend read Matthew 18:15-20. The "two or three" mentioned in this passage also has to do with discipline. Normally it is not used that way.

RECEIVE

DAY 2

1 Corinthians 5:5

5 Then you must throw this man out and hand him over to Satan so that his sinful nature will be destroyed and he himself will be saved on the day the Lord returns.

Paul told the church what to do: they were to expel this man from their fellowship. Notice that the ultimate recovery of this person is intended. The purpose of discipline should not be to punish, but to restore. Paul wanted this person to be brought to the ruin of his sin nature but did not think this would cause him to lose his salvation. Paul wanted him to "be saved on the day the Lord returns."

REFLECT

In times when you have seen discipline exercised, was the goal recovery?

RESPOND

Read Hebrews 12:5-11 to see that God disciplines His children. As older children look back on their lives they usually realize what their parents did was for their good, not just for the sake of punishment.

RECEIVE

DAY 3

1 Corinthians 5:6-8

[6] Your boasting about this is terrible. Don't you realize that this sin is like a little yeast that spreads through the whole batch of dough? [7] Get rid of the old "yeast" by removing this wicked person from among you. Then you will be like a fresh batch of dough made without yeast, which is what you really are. Christ, our Passover Lamb, has been sacrificed for us. [8] So let us celebrate the festival, not with the old bread of wickedness and evil, but with the new bread of sincerity and truth.

Just as yeast could grow and effect the entire loaf, a little sin could have the effect of growing and causing problems for the entire church body. He referred to the believers' position in Christ when he wrote, "without yeast, which is what you really are." Now he wanted them to live out in practice what their position in Christ was.

REFLECT

Is it your desire to live out what your position in Christ is?

RESPOND

For your position in Christ, join with a friend in reading Ephesians 2:6-7. This passage reveals the position of believers in Jesus. Their desire should be to show that in their daily lives.

RECEIVE

DAY 4

1 Corinthians 5:9-10

⁹ When I wrote to you before, I told you not to associate with people who indulge in sexual sin. ¹⁰ But I wasn't talking about unbelievers who indulge in sexual sin, or are greedy, or cheat people, or worship idols. You would have to leave this world to avoid people like that.

Biblical separation has been debated by many. In this passage, Paul tells of those from whom believers are to be separated. Paul said a believer could not be completely separated from unbelievers or the believer would have to go out of this world. There is no way to avoid unbelievers as one lives in this world.

REFLECT

Do you realize you cannot be completely separated from unbelievers? Think of the professional people caring for you. Several are likely not believers in Jesus.

RESPOND

Seek to be a witness to your care givers who may not be believers. Develop a short comment of no more than a minute that you can memorize and be ready to give whenever the opportunity arises. Even on business calls when they ask at the end if there's anything else, you could say, "Yes, please give me less than a minute to tell you what Jesus means to me." Then proceed immediately telling your story. Some may let you know they are also believers in Jesus. If there is no response, you have at least planted a seed for them to think about.

DAY 5

RECEIVE

1 Corinthians 5:11

¹¹ I meant that you are not to associate with anyone who claims to be a believer yet indulges in sexual sin, or is greedy, or worships idols, or is abusive, or is a drunkard, or cheats people. Don't even eat with such people.

In this passage Paul tells of those from whom believers in Jesus are to be separated. Those who can mar your testimony are not unbelievers, but believers who are living like unbelievers. Notice the list Paul gave for those from whom you should separate: "Anyone who claims to be a believer yet indulges in sexual sin, or is greedy, or worships idols, or is abusive, or is a drunkard, or cheats people."

REFLECT

Does this cause you to think about your friends? Do some fall into one of these categories? If so, what should you do?

RESPOND

Because believers in Jesus have the Holy Spirit living in them, each one is a temple of God. With a friend read 2 Corinthians 6:16-18 to see how this should influence the way a believer lives.

WEEK 11:
1 CORINTHIANS 5, 6

RECEIVE

1 Corinthians 5:12-13

[12] It isn't my responsibility to judge outsiders, but it certainly is your responsibility to judge those inside the church who are sinning. [13] God will judge those on the outside; but as the Scriptures say, "You must remove the evil person from among you."

By "outsiders" Paul referred to those outside the local church assembly. On the other hand, he emphasized it was their duty to judge (evaluate) those inside the church. He said nothing about judging motives. He was concerned they go by actions. Because a person who called himself a believer was living in sin, Paul said he should be removed from their midst.

REFLECT

Does it comfort you to know that it is not your responsibility to judge those outside the church?

RESPOND

With a friend consider a passage where Paul suggested those in the church should contact those outside the church. The passage is 1 Timothy 3:6-7 that tells about qualifications for selecting church leaders. Such candidates should be well spoken of in the community.

RECEIVE

DAY 2

1 Corinthians 6:1-3

¹ When one of you has a dispute with another believer, how dare you file a lawsuit and ask a secular court to decide the matter instead of taking it to other believers! ² Don't you realize that someday we believers will judge the world? And since you are going to judge the world, can't you decide even these little things among yourselves? ³ Don't you realize that we will judge angels? So you should surely be able to resolve ordinary disputes in this life.

Paul wrote to the Corinthian believers about how to solve differences of opinion among their members. When there was open sin, the person involved should be expelled from the church group. 1 Corinthians 6 has to do with differences of opinion that some were taking to court to have resolved. Paul considered their problems to be "ordinary disputes" in contrast to what believers would be doing in eternity. See Jude 1:6 for angels being judged.

REFLECT

Do you know of situations that would have been better settled inside your church rather than on the outside?

RESPOND

Pray for Christian organizations that sometimes may have the right to sue but decide not to because of the bad publicity it would produce. They choose rather to suffer loss.

RECEIVE

1 Corinthians 6:4-6

⁴ If you have legal disputes about such matters, why go to outside judges who are not respected by the church? ⁵ I am saying this to shame you. Isn't there anyone in all the church who is wise enough to decide these issues? ⁶ But instead, one believer sues another—right in front of unbelievers!

Paul was concerned about the testimony of the church in the community. Permitting judges who are not Christ followers to decide a dispute between believers would harm the church's testimony. Paul was horrified at the idea that believers would take a case to be settled by unbelievers.

REFLECT

Have you seen this kind of thing occurring in your local assembly? What was the impression of others about this?

RESPOND

Discuss with a Christian friend what your action will be if you ever face such a situation as Paul described. Will you go to court before unbelievers or ask those in your local church to act as judges over the matter?

RECEIVE

DAY 4

1 Corinthians 6:7–8

[7] Even to have such lawsuits with one another is a defeat for you. Why not just accept the injustice and leave it at that? Why not let yourselves be cheated? [8] Instead, you yourselves are the ones who do wrong and cheat even your fellow believers.

Paul urged the believers in Corinth—and all believers by inspiration of the Scriptures—to accept being cheated rather than going before those outside the church. Paul said that they themselves were cheaters if they took fellow believers to a court outside the church. No one likes to accept an injustice, but Paul said it should be done for the sake of the testimony of the church.

REFLECT

Have you thought about these matters before? Have Paul's instructions been helpful to you in deciding what you would do if such an occasion arose in your life?

RESPOND

Visit with a friend about what Jesus said as recorded in John 13:34–35. Would those in your community say this is true of your church fellowship?

RECEIVE

DAY 5

1 Corinthians 6:9-11

⁹ Don't you realize that those who do wrong will not inherit the Kingdom of God? Don't fool yourselves. Those who indulge in sexual sin, or who worship idols, or commit adultery, or are male prostitutes, or practice homosexuality, ¹⁰ or are thieves, or greedy people, or drunkards, or are abusive, or cheat people— none of these will inherit the Kingdom of God. ¹¹ Some of you were once like that. But you were cleansed; you were made holy; you were made right with God by calling on the name of the Lord Jesus Christ and by the Spirit of our God.

Paul described the kinds of habitual sins that would cause one not to be able to be in God's kingdom. The Roman Empire and the city of Corinth were known for all kinds of immorality and corruption. One author says that 14 of the first 15 Roman emperors of the empire were homosexual or bisexual. Some of these Corinthian believers were like those mentioned in Paul's list, but their lives had been changed by believing in Jesus as Savior.

REFLECT

Think about the changes Jesus has made in your life after you received Him as Savior. Share your testimony with others.

RESPOND

Visit with a friend about the change that Paul said had occurred in the lives of the Corinthians after they received Jesus as Savior. Discuss how this is a different message than one normally hears from society today.

WEEK 12:
1 CORINTHIANS 6, 7

1 Corinthians 6:12

¹² You say, "I am allowed to do anything"—but not everything is good for you. And even though "I am allowed to do anything," I must not become a slave to anything.

Paul writes about Christian liberty. Although a person who trusts in Jesus as Savior is saved by His grace apart from law, this does not mean the person can live like a lawless individual. Before salvation the person was a slave to sin. After salvation he or she should not become a slave to other things.

REFLECT

Have you thought of your salvation being a love relationship with the Lord Jesus? You should not want to do anything that would displease Him.

RESPOND

With a friend read 2 Corinthians 4:16-18. This passage aids believers in fixing their eyes on that which is eternal rather than just on that which is temporal.

RECEIVE

DAY 2

1 Corinthians 6:13-14

[13] You say, "Food was made for the stomach, and the stomach for food." (This is true, though someday God will do away with both of them.) But you can't say that our bodies were made for sexual immorality. They were made for the Lord, and the Lord cares about our bodies. [14] And God will raise us from the dead by his power, just as he raised our Lord from the dead.

Paul again warned about sexual immorality. The believer's body is inhabited by the Holy Spirit and in this sense is "made for the Lord." The believer can be assured of his or her future resurrection just as God raised Jesus from the dead. Believers serve a miracle-working God.

REFLECT

Regardless of what you physically experience in this life, as a believer your body will someday be raised from the dead. In the meantime, honor the Lord with your body.

RESPOND

Join with a friend in reading 1 Thessalonians 4:13-18. This passage assures believers about someday being raised from the dead.

RECEIVE

DAY 3

1 Corinthians 6:15-17

¹⁵ Don't you realize that your bodies are actually parts of Christ? Should a man take his body, which is part of Christ, and join it to a prostitute? Never! ¹⁶ And don't you realize that if a man joins himself to a prostitute, he becomes one body with her? For the Scriptures say, "The two are united into one." ¹⁷ But the person who is joined to the Lord is one spirit with him.

Paul told why one who is part of Jesus should not become part of one who is not. Paul quoted from Genesis 2:24 in saying that in such a relationship the two become one. That should be reserved for the marriage relationship, in which God intended the uniting of one man and one woman.

REFLECT

Notice how often the writers of the New Testament referred to the Old Testament. This indicates both are inspired by God.

RESPOND

With a friend examine the passages of 2 Timothy 3:16-17 and 2 Peter 1:20-21. These passages reveal God breathed out the message He wanted the human authors to write.

RECEIVE

1 Corinthians 6:18-20

[18] Run from sexual sin! No other sin so clearly affects the body as this one does. For sexual immorality is a sin against your own body. [19] Don't you realize that your body is the temple of the Holy Spirit, who lives in you and was given to you by God? You do not belong to yourself, [20] for God bought you with a high price. So you must honor God with your body.

Paul continued to warn about sexual sin and wanted believers to run from it. With the known disease that results from sexual sin it is seen that this is a sin against one's own body. Paul reminded the believers that their bodies were the temple of the Holy Spirit. Because the Holy Spirit inhabited their bodies, they should honor God with their bodies.

REFLECT

Have you known before that the Holy Spirit inhabits your body when you trust in Jesus as Savior?

RESPOND

Study the passages with a friend that tells about the Holy Spirit inhabiting the believer's body. See Romans 8:9 and 1 Corinthians 12:13. Think how the Jews respected the physical temple; it's an example of the way believers in Jesus should respect their bodies.

RECEIVE

DAY 5

1 Corinthians 7:1-2

[1] Now regarding the questions you asked in your letter. Yes, it is good to abstain from sexual relations. [2] But because there is so much sexual immorality, each man should have his own wife, and each woman should have her own husband.

The Corinthian believers had written a letter to Paul with several questions. One had to do with sexual relations and marriage. 1 Corinthians 7 contains many instructions in answer to this question. It is a passage that is referred to today in counseling single and married people. It is inspired by God and has been of help to many.

REFLECT

Think how practical the Bible is in that it deals with problems commonly faced. It is like an instruction book on how to live the Christian life.

RESPOND

Recommend 1 Corinthians 7 to people today who have the same questions the believers in Corinth asked the apostle Paul. The apostle not only knew what Jesus had said when He was on earth but also what He had revealed to him after he became an apostle.

WEEK 13:
1 CORINTHIANS 7

RECEIVE

1 Corinthians 7:3-4

[3] The husband should fulfill his wife's sexual needs, and the wife should fulfill her husband's needs. [4] The wife gives authority over her body to her husband, and the husband gives authority over his body to his wife.

These are Paul's instructions for mutual satisfaction in the husband/ wife relationship. Some discuss whether Paul himself was married. Further verses in 1 Corinthians 7 seem at this time he was not. He had been a member of the Sanhedrin (the Jewish Supreme court). Some believe he had to be married to be qualified for that position. At the time he wrote this he may have been a widower. He could speak from experience as well as revelation.

REFLECT

When needing counsel about marriage, it is good to go to a godly couple who is married or to someone who has had a successful marriage but now may be a widow or widower.

RESPOND

With a friend read Proverbs 27:9-10. You need counsel from someone who understands your heart's needs. Sometimes that can be from one who is a brother or sister in Christ rather than a biological family member.

RECEIVE

DAY 2

1 Corinthians 7:5

⁵ Do not deprive each other of sexual relations, unless you both agree to refrain from sexual intimacy for a limited time so you can give yourselves more completely to prayer. Afterward, you should come together again so that Satan won't be able to tempt you because of your lack of self-control.

Corinth was a wicked city and sex was part of its religion. Christian couples could be confused about what was previously heard and were in need of being taught the proper place of sexual intimacy between married couples. Marriage and sex were God's idea, but he created such for those who love Him and want to honor Him in their marriage.

REFLECT

Think how blessed believers are that the Lord has provided the Bible to give practical instructions for how believers should live and relate to each other.

RESPOND

For the way a husband and wife should relate to each other, read Ephesians 5:21-33. This short passage has many instructions for married life.

RECEIVE

DAY 3

1 Corinthians 7:6-7

[6] I say this as a concession, not as a command. [7] But I wish everyone were single, just as I am. Yet each person has a special gift from God, of one kind or another.

Verse 7 is the verse that indicates Paul was single at the time he wrote this. Although he preferred others would lead a celibate life as he was doing, he was not commanding it. He recognized that "each person has a special gift from God." Paul did not want to press everyone into the same mold.

REFLECT

Do you recognize that God has gifted people differently so they do not all need to act in the same way?

RESPOND

Paul will go into detail in 1 Corinthians 12 about spiritual gifts given by God to His people. With a friend read some other passages that tell about spiritual gifts. See Romans 12:6-8; Ephesians 4:11-13; 1 Peter 4:10-11.

RECEIVE

1 Corinthians 7:8-9

⁸ So I say to those who aren't married and to widows—it's better to stay unmarried, just as I am. ⁹ But if they can't control themselves, they should go ahead and marry. It's better to marry than to burn with lust.

Paul mentioned again what his marital state was. He recognized that not everyone should remain single. Some would be able to control their desires; others could not so it was better for them to marry.

REFLECT

Notice how considerate the apostle Paul was in thinking of those different than he was.

RESPOND

Visit with a friend about being considerate of people who face problems you do not face. Have a compassion for others. By doing so you will follow the example of your heavenly Father seen in Luke 6:35-36.

RECEIVE

DAY 5

1 Corinthians 7:10-11

¹⁰ But for those who are married, I have a command that comes not from me, but from the Lord. A wife must not leave her husband. ¹¹ But if she does leave him, let her remain single or else be reconciled to him. And the husband must not leave his wife.

Paul wrote that his command to those married comes from the Lord. For a passage that records what Jesus said see Mark 10:11-12. Paul seems to refer to separation in 1 Corinthians 7:10-11 rather than divorce. Separation would allow for a time of reconciliation after which they could come back together.

REFLECT

There are several views about separation and divorce. Be confident your desires are to please the Lord and not yourself.

RESPOND

Use a passage such as Colossians 1:9-10 in decisions you must make. When wondering which way to turn, use Colossians 3:15 as a guide. Let the peace of God rule (call the decision) in your life.

WEEK 14:
1 CORINTHIANS 7

RECEIVE

1 Corinthians 7:12-13

[12] Now, I will speak to the rest of you, though I do not have a direct command from the Lord. If a fellow believer has a wife who is not a believer and she is willing to continue living with him, he must not leave her. [13] And if a believing woman has a husband who is not a believer and he is willing to continue living with her, she must not leave him.

Paul dealt with what should occur in a marriage if one becomes a believer and the other is not. If the unbeliever is willing to continue living with the believer, then that should be allowed. Paul first used the husband in his example and then used a wife to say the same. Paul was concerned that such marriages should not be ended if the unbeliever is willing to live with the believer.

REFLECT

Often we think the problem of being unequally yoked is only with whom one marries. Have you thought about what to do if the problem arises after marriage?

RESPOND

The matter of being unequally yoked has to do with a believer not marrying an unbeliever. This is treated in 2 Corinthians 6:14-15. In 1 Corinthians 7:12-13 Paul gave instructions about this occurring after marriage. Talk with a friend about the differences in these situations.

RECEIVE

1 Corinthians 7:14

¹⁴ For the believing wife brings holiness to her marriage, and the believing husband brings holiness to his marriage. Otherwise, your children would not be holy, but now they are holy.

Paul now answers why he gave permission for an unbeliever to remain with a believer if this unequal yoke occurred after marriage. The words "holiness" and "holy" are related to the same Greek word for "sanctification" and "sanctify." The meaning in both cases refers to being "set apart." If the unbeliever will remain with the believer, the children are "set apart" in a better situation than if the couple ended their marriage.

REFLECT

Thank the Lord that, as a believer in Jesus, you are set apart from the things of the world to serve and honor Him.

RESPOND

Visit with a friend about how Paul's letter began in 1 Corinthians 1:2. He referred to the believers as "holy people." See what this verse says about how they were made that way.

RECEIVE

DAY 3

1 Corinthians 7:15-16

[15] (But if the husband or wife who isn't a believer insists on leaving, let them go. In such cases the believing husband or wife is no longer bound to the other, for God has called you to live in peace.) [16] Don't you wives realize that your husbands might be saved because of you? And don't you husbands realize that your wives might be saved because of you?

If the unsaved spouse insists on leaving, the other spouse should let the person leave. Paul did not want a person to have to live in an abusive household; instead he said, "God has called you to live in peace." If the unsaved person would stay with the believing spouse, that could result in the salvation of the unbeliever. This would have an eternal benefit.

REFLECT

This points out the concern every believer should have for unbelievers. All a Christ follower can do is live out the life of Christ. Only God can convert the unsaved person.

RESPOND

Join with a friend to read what the apostle Peter said about wives winning their husbands as he wrote 1 Peter 3:1-2. A changed life is one of the greatest testimonies to an unsaved spouse or other unbelievers.

RECEIVE

1 Corinthians 7:17

¹⁷ Each of you should continue to live in whatever situation the Lord has placed you, and remain as you were when God first called you. This is my rule for all the churches.

Paul had said that a believer should permit an unbeliever to stay in the marriage relationship. He further instructed that people should remain in the situation they were in when they trusted Jesus as Savior. In this case it meant they should not seek a divorce even though they are now unequally yoked together.

REFLECT

What kind of a situation were you in when you trusted Jesus as Savior? Did you remain as you had been?

RESPOND

It does not seem the apostle was saying a person should stay in an ungodly business after trusting in Jesus as Savior. If the believer wishes to honor Christ in all he or she does, it will not be long before the person will know what they should do.

RECEIVE

DAY 5

1 Corinthians 7:18-19

18 For instance, a man who was circumcised before he became a believer should not try to reverse it. And the man who was uncircumcised when he became a believer should not be circumcised now. 19 For it makes no difference whether or not a man has been circumcised. The important thing is to keep God's commandments.

Paul wrote about the distinction of Jews and Gentiles. After salvation, the individual should not try to change his nationality. The most important thing was to live in a way that honors God. Born again Jews should seek to win others to Christ (Messiah), and Gentiles should seek to win others to Him also.

REFLECT

How has your life changed since you trusted in Jesus for salvation? Have you told others this?

RESPOND

Your attitude toward others will be an example that you are a Christ follower. Believers had been told they should love each other, but notice the "new commandment" Jesus gave them in John 13:34. Discuss with a friend about what makes this commandment a new one.

WEEK 15:
1 CORINTHIANS 7

RECEIVE

1 Corinthians 7:20-22

20 Yes, each of you should remain as you were when God called you. 21 Are you a slave? Don't let that worry you—but if you get a chance to be free, take it. 22 And remember, if you were a slave when the Lord called you, you are now free in the Lord. And if you were free when the Lord called you, you are now a slave of Christ.

Paul emphasized how believers should stay in their present situation at the time they trusted in Jesus as Savior. Even a slave should continue as he was but realize he is free in Jesus. The slave needed to realize that his master had changed from an earthly one to a heavenly one.

REFLECT

Do you realize that if you have trusted in Jesus as Savior that now "you are a slave of Christ"? It is a love relationship unlike what earthly slaves had.

RESPOND

Join with a friend in reading Ephesians 6:5-8. This passage also tells about how the perspective of slaves should change after they have trusted in Jesus for salvation. Talk with your friend about how this applies to the employee/employer relationship.

RECEIVE

1 Corinthians 7:23-24

²³ God paid a high price for you, so don't be enslaved by the world. ²⁴ Each of you, dear brothers and sisters, should remain as you were when God first called you.

Earthly slaves knew all about their masters paying a price for them. This transferred them from one earthly master to another one. Paul used this example to remind them that God had paid a high price for them so they should not let people enslave them. Again Paul reminded them to "remain as you were when God first called you."

REFLECT

Think about the high price God paid for you. It was by sending His own Son to die on the cross for you. Now you have a new Master because you belong to Jesus after trusting in Him.

RESPOND

The slaves were aware of the Greek word for "buy" in regard to being bought in the market place. Greek also put a preposition on front of the word that meant "out of" or "from." It would refer to them being bought out of the market place of sin. The word is used in Galatians 3:13 and 4:5 referring to being bought out from under the penalty of the law.

RECEIVE

1 Corinthians 7:25

[25] Now regarding your question about the young women who are not yet married. I do not have a command from the Lord for them. But the Lord in his mercy has given me wisdom that can be trusted, and I will share it with you.

Paul turned to answer another question the Corinthian believers had asked him. It had to do with young unmarried women. Some take this to refer to all young single women; others take this to refer to a father of a young single daughter. Should he give her away in marriage or not? Paul did not have a direct command from Jesus about this, but as an apostle writing by inspiration he could share his counsel.

REFLECT

Perhaps you have wondered about the same question the Christians were asking Paul. If so, you will be interested in his answer.

RESPOND

Visit with a friend about how to counsel young women who may wonder about the question Paul is about to answer. This shows how practical the topics in 1 Corinthians 7 are today.

RECEIVE

DAY 4

1 Corinthians 7:26-28

[26] Because of the present crisis, I think it is best to remain as you are. [27] If you have a wife, do not seek to end the marriage. If you do not have a wife, do not seek to get married. [28] But if you do get married, it is not a sin. And if a young woman gets married, it is not a sin. However, those who get married at this time will have troubles, and I am trying to spare you those problems.

Paul gave his reasons for the unmarried to stay as they were. He was concerned about the condition of society around them. As mentioned previously, Corinth was a sex-saturated society with all kinds of immorality. Some think it could not have been worse than current conditions today, but his counsel would apply to today also.

REFLECT

Whatever your marital status today, Paul's advice remains spiritually wise.

RESPOND

Paul was giving practical advice when he said that those who get married will have troubles. Each believer should desire to place God first in life, but marriage adds an element that detracts many, as the present divorce rate shows. Both mates need to keep God first place in life.

DAY 5

RECEIVE

1 Corinthians 7:29-31

²⁹ But let me say this, dear brothers and sisters: The time that remains is very short. So from now on, those with wives should not focus only on their marriage. ³⁰ Those who weep or who rejoice or who buy things should not be absorbed by their weeping or their joy or their possessions. ³¹ Those who use the things of the world should not become attached to them. For this world as we know it will soon pass away.

Paul gave reasons for his counsel about marriage. The time is short, he said. Notice that he expected the Lord could return for believers at any time. He was not thinking prophecies had to be fulfilled before that time. If that was true in his time, think of how much shorter the time is now. He also warned about not being absorbed in the world's possessions because they would soon pass away. Although believers are in the world and have possessions, they should not permit the things of the world to possess them. God is to be first in their lives.

REFLECT

Think of the complexities of life and how they compete with the believer desiring to put God first.

RESPOND

With a friend read 1 Thessalonians 4:13-18. This passage tells about Jesus returning in the air to bring back with Him believers who have died. Their glorified bodies will be brought forth at that time. It also tells of the catching up (rapture) of believers living at that time.

WEEK 16:
1 CORINTHIANS 7, 8

RECEIVE

1 Corinthians 7:32-34

[32] I want you to be free from the concerns of this life. An unmarried man can spend his time doing the Lord's work and thinking how to please him. [33] But a married man has to think about his earthly responsibilities and how to please his wife. [34] His interests are divided. In the same way, a woman who is no longer married or has never been married can be devoted to the Lord and holy in body and in spirit. But a married woman has to think about her earthly responsibilities and how to please her husband.

Paul continued his counsel for the unmarried. Whether it involves a man or a woman, the extra cares of marriage take time away from serving the Lord. It becomes a divided loyalty between serving and pleasing one's mate with the earthly responsibilities, or having only the Lord to serve and please.

REFLECT

Talk with a few couples about Paul's counsel. It has to be taken along with the other comments he made in this chapter.

RESPOND

Visit with a friend about what 1 Corinthians 7:32-34 is saying. Talk about how it can be used in talking with others asking questions that relate to this passage.

RECEIVE

DAY 2

1 Corinthians 7:35

[35] I am saying this for your benefit, not to place restrictions on you. I want you to do whatever will help you serve the Lord best, with as few distractions as possible.

Occasionally it is thought that the instructions in the Bible are limiting us. Paul reminded his readers that the restrictions he was mentioning were for their good. He wanted them to have as few distractions as possible as they lived to please the Lord.

REFLECT

Think of the commandments and instructions in the Bible as being for your benefit. They are not unnecessary restrictions taking away your pleasure for living.

RESPOND

The 23rd Psalm is a favorite of most Christians. Notice what verse 6 says in this psalm. Do you believe it?

RECEIVE

1 Corinthians 7:36-38

[36] But if a man thinks that he's treating his fiancée improperly and will inevitably give in to his passion, let him marry her as he wishes. It is not a sin. [37] But if he has decided firmly not to marry and there is no urgency and he can control his passion, he does well not to marry. [38] So the person who marries his fiancée does well, and the person who doesn't marry does even better.

Paul described the two kinds of men—one kind who can control passions; one who cannot. Being single can honor God and being married can honor Him. Paul thought the one who did not marry was in the better situation. The state of singleness or marriage could each honor God.

REFLECT

Be careful in thinking that either singleness or marriage is more spiritual than the other.

RESPOND

A primary passage referring to what a Christian marriage should be like is described in Ephesians 5:21-33. Many overlook verse 21 as they seek to explain the passage. A Christian marriage should reflect what Christ's relation is to the church. Submission does not imply enduring abuse.

RECEIVE

1 Corinthians 7:39-40

[39] A wife is bound to her husband as long as he lives. If her husband dies, she is free to marry anyone she wishes, but only if he loves the Lord. [40] But in my opinion it would be better for her to stay single, and I think I am giving you counsel from God's Spirit when I say this.

Paul instructed what the Christian wife is to do if her husband dies. She is free to marry another Christ follower. Paul would prefer, however, that she remain single. This is based on the previous remarks he stated in this chapter.

REFLECT

Paul considered marriage to be for one man and one woman until death. But he gave instructions about what should be done after the death of a mate.

RESPOND

For a corresponding passage, also written by the apostle Paul, read Romans 7:1-4. Discuss this passage with a friend.

RECEIVE

DAY 5

1 Corinthians 8:1

[1] Now regarding your question about food that has been offered to idols. Yes, we know that "we all have knowledge" about this issue. But while knowledge makes us feel important, it is love that strengthens the church.

Paul turned his attention toward answering another question the Corinthian believers had asked him. This dealt with meat that had been offered to idols. Apparently the best had been offered and the remains were placed in the marketplace. Some believers were buying that good meat that had been offered to idols, realizing that an idol is nothing. This was confusing to those saved out of idol worship who thought the practice of the believers was being involved with idols.

REFLECT

Have you had a new believer become confused because of something you do that he did not understand?

RESPOND

Visit with a friend about how your actions may be confusing to some new believers. Use Ephesians 5:15 as an example as to how Christ followers should live. It matters what others think.

WEEK 17:
1 CORINTHIANS 8

RECEIVE

1 Corinthians 8:2-3

² Anyone who claims to know all the answers doesn't really know very much. ³ But the person who loves God is the one whom God recognizes.

This is a sobering reminder for those who think they have all the answers. Knowledge is important because there are many things one needs to know about God from the Scriptures. Knowledge without love, however, will harm more people than it will help. The context, remember, has to do with eating meat that has been offered to idols. Those with knowledge should not put stumbling blocks in front of new believers in Jesus.

REFLECT

Are you concerned about those who have recently trusted in Jesus as Savior? Do you have a burden to help them along in the Christian life?

RESPOND

Talk with a fellow believer about the importance of being involved in a local church fellowship. Read Hebrews 10:24-25 in this regard. Sadly there are those who want to be a part of the family of God by believing in Jesus but do not want to have anything to do with the family. This is not what God intended.

RECEIVE

DAY 2

1 Corinthians 8:4–5

[4] So, what about eating meat that has been offered to idols? Well, we all know that an idol is not really a god and that there is only one God. [5] There may be so-called gods both in heaven and on earth, and some people actually worship many gods and many lords.

By the mature believer's knowledge, he knows that an idol does not really represent a true God. The unbeliever or even a new believer in Jesus may not know this. Because of this, Paul was writing to help more mature believers know how to act around those immature ones without this knowledge.

REFLECT

Have you had the privilege of being a spiritual mentor to a new believer? If so, God is enabling you to be a spiritual parent to that person.

RESPOND

Join with a Christian friend to ask God to enable you to be a spiritual mentor to a new believer. Some have said that every Paul needs a Timothy and every Timothy needs a Paul. Read 1 Timothy 1:2 to see how Paul referred to Timothy. It is likely that Timothy's believing mother led him to the Lord (see Acts 16:1-2), but Paul mentored him like a son.

RECEIVE

DAY 3

1 Corinthians 8:6-7

⁶ But for us, there is one God, the Father, by whom all things were created, and for whom we live. And there is one Lord, Jesus Christ, through whom all things were created, and through whom we live. ⁷ However, not all believers know this. Some are accustomed to thinking of idols as being real, so when they eat food that has been offered to idols, they think of it as the worship of real gods, and their weak consciences are violated.

Paul contrasted what knowledgeable believers know in contrast to what other believers do not know. Some young believers are ignorant; that is, they are unaware of what the Scriptures teach about the true God and false gods. They are also unaware of the liberty they have in Jesus. Because of this, they think that more mature believers eating meat offered to idols are guilty of worshiping a false god.

REFLECT

The Bible is the only book God has inspired. Are you engaged in it by listening to it or reading it at least four times a week? This will make a significant difference in your life.

RESPOND

Back to the Bible's research has shown that those engaged in the Bible at least four times a week have a decrease in bad habits and an increase in godly habits. Talk with a friend about being engaged in the Bible by reading or listening to it at least four times a week.

RECEIVE

DAY 4

1 Corinthians 8:8–9

[8] It's true that we can't win God's approval by what we eat. We don't lose anything if we don't eat it, and we don't gain anything if we do. [9] But you must be careful so that your freedom does not cause others with a weaker conscience to stumble.

Paul minimized the importance of the meat problem the Corinthians were struggling with. He wanted the mature believers to know that it was better for them to bypass getting some good meat at perhaps a better price if doing so would be a problem to a less mature and less knowledgeable believer.

REFLECT

Are this passage and the comments about it helping you to think about some of the things you are doing? Could a new believer misunderstand some of your actions?

RESPOND

Visit about this issue with a friend. Sometimes mature believers who are legalists will act offended like a weaker Christian. It may be the case that even the mature believer has not been properly taught the Scriptures on such matters. If a knowledgeable believer realizes an action could be misunderstood by a new believer, love for the brother in Christ should cause him not to do it.

DAY 5

RECEIVE

1 Corinthians 8:10-11

[10] For if others see you—with your "superior knowledge"—eating in the temple of an idol, won't they be encouraged to violate their conscience by eating food that has been offered to an idol? [11] So because of your superior knowledge, a weak believer for whom Christ died will be destroyed.

Apparently families could gather in an area of the temple for a meal or activities such as weddings. If a new believer saw a mature believer eating in the temple of an idol, the new believer might think the mature one was guilty of idol worship. The new believer might be "destroyed" in the sense that this would arrest his spiritual growth.

REFLECT

Have you found today that some believers are still living as if they were under the Old Testament law?

RESPOND

Visit with a friend about the apostle Paul. Before his salvation he was a Jewish Pharisee and kept the Old Testament law. After he became a believer in Jesus he wrote Colossians 2:16-17 about not judging anyone based on diet or holy days. Are you following Paul's instructions? Believers need to be taught such passages.

WEEK 18:
1 CORINTHIANS 8, 9

RECEIVE

1 Corinthians 8:12-13

[12] And when you sin against other believers by encouraging them to do something they believe is wrong, you are sinning against Christ. [13] So if what I eat causes another believer to sin, I will never eat meat again as long as I live—for I don't want to cause another believer to stumble.

A person is not to go against his or her conscience. The conscience could be wrong but until there is proper teaching the person should not go against it. The "weaker" believer in this situation was an untaught believer. When Paul mentioned not eating meat again, the context referred to meat offered to idols.

REFLECT

Would you feel as strongly as the apostle Paul if you thought your actions were causing a new, untaught believer to stumble in his Christian faith?

RESPOND

Visit with a friend about the importance of taking others into consideration as you live to please Jesus. Read what the apostle Paul wrote in Romans 14:12-15 as he wrote about being a good witness to others.

DAY 2

RECEIVE

1 Corinthians 9:1-2

¹ Am I not as free as anyone else? Am I not an apostle? Haven't I seen Jesus our Lord with my own eyes? Isn't it because of my work that you belong to the Lord? ² Even if others think I am not an apostle, I certainly am to you. You yourselves are proof that I am the Lord's apostle.

Paul gave himself as an example of someone who had Christian liberty. He introduced the topic by establishing his authority as he wrote to the Corinthian church. Apparently some in the area doubted he was a true apostle. He had seen the resurrected Lord with his own eyes. What Paul had done for the believers there was proof of his apostleship.

REFLECT

Do you realize how blessed you are to have a copy of the apostle Paul's writing in the Scriptures?

RESPOND

Paul was not qualified to be one of the 12 apostles after Judas betrayed Jesus. See the qualifications needed in Acts 1:21-22. Paul saw the risen Lord when he was converted as he traveled the road to Damascus (see Acts 9:1-9).

RECEIVE

DAY 3

1 Corinthians 9:3-6

³ This is my answer to those who question my authority. ⁴ Don't we have the right to live in your homes and share your meals? ⁵ Don't we have the right to bring a believing wife with us as the other apostles and the Lord's brothers do, and as Peter does? ⁶ Or is it only Barnabas and I who have to work to support ourselves?

Paul told about the rights he had if he chose to exercise them. Notice he referred to Peter's wife in contrast to those who do not think he was married. Paul and Barnabas worked to support themselves, but he wanted it known it could have been their right to expect support from those whom they served.

REFLECT

Do you sometimes give up some right you have in order to be a good testimony to others?

RESPOND

For those who wonder if the apostle Peter was married, see also Matthew 8:14-15. Visit with a friend about being willing to give up a right you have if it would be a good testimony to some new but untaught believer.

RECEIVE

1 Corinthians 9:7–8

[7] What soldier has to pay his own expenses? What farmer plants a vineyard and doesn't have the right to eat some of its fruit? What shepherd cares for a flock of sheep and isn't allowed to drink some of the milk? [8] Am I expressing merely a human opinion, or does the law say the same thing?

Paul continued to talk about the right others had to benefit from something they were doing. He even appealed to the law in making his case about benefitting from the work one does. What do you imagine the people were thinking by the time they came this far in reading his letter?

REFLECT

Consider that those who teach the Bible should receive something for doing so. For some it is only done occasionally; for others it is a full-time ministry.

RESPOND

Visit with a fellow believer about the need to contribute material means to someone from whom you are being spiritually nourished. This would also apply to a church from which you receive spiritual nourishment.

DAY 5

RECEIVE

1 Corinthians 9:9-10

[9] For the law of Moses says, "You must not muzzle an ox to keep it from eating as it treads out the grain." Was God thinking only about oxen when he said this? [10] Wasn't he actually speaking to us? Yes, it was written for us, so that the one who plows and the one who threshes the grain might both expect a share of the harvest.

Paul cited the Old Testament law to show the principle of a worker being worthy of financial support. The worker, or even an animal, was to share in the harvest. Those in full-time ministry, such as traveling evangelists, need to have their expenses met as well as an honorarium for their ministry. If they don't receive such they will eventually not be able to travel and minister.

REFLECT

Consider how carefully your church group reimburses a special speaker brought to your church. Will what it gives help continue the person's ministry or reduce it?

RESPOND

This was not the only time the apostle Paul cited the Old Testament instructions about the ox at harvest time (see 1 Timothy 5:17-18). Paul was making the point that one who spends his life sharing the gospel should be supported by those who are benefitting from it.

WEEK 19:
1 CORINTHIANS 9

DAY 1

1 Corinthians 9:11-12

[11] Since we have planted spiritual seed among you, aren't we entitled to a harvest of physical food and drink? [12] If you support others who preach to you, shouldn't we have an even greater right to be supported? But we have never used this right. We would rather put up with anything than be an obstacle to the Good News about Christ.

Paul drove his point home about the ministry he and Barnabas had among the Corinthian believers. Apparently the believers were supporting others but not Paul and Barnabas. Paul said they had never used this right because they did not want to be a stumbling block to those to whom they were presenting the gospel.

REFLECT

Have you previously thought about what the apostle Paul said in 1 Corinthians 9:11-12?

RESPOND

Visit with a friend about this passage in 1 Corinthians and then discuss how you are, or are not, doing this.

RECEIVE

1 Corinthians 9:13-14

¹³ Don't you realize that those who work in the temple get their meals from the offerings brought to the temple? And those who serve at the altar get a share of the sacrificial offerings. ¹⁴ In the same way, the Lord ordered that those who preach the Good News should be supported by those who benefit from it.

Paul continued to drive home his point by citing the Old Testament law system. The Corinthians may have known this practice was also followed in the pagan temples of their time. Paul's statement is strong when he wrote, "In the same way, the Lord ordered that those who preach the Good News should be supported by those who benefit from it."

REFLECT

Do you agree that some statements in the Bible are clear without further debate?

RESPOND

Discuss with a friend about the Old Testament instructions about how the priests and Levites were to be supported. Read Numbers 18:8-11 to help in your discussion.

RECEIVE

1 Corinthians 9:15-16

[15] Yet I have never used any of these rights. And I am not writing this to suggest that I want to start now. In fact, I would rather die than lose my right to boast about preaching without charge. [16] Yet preaching the Good News is not something I can boast about. I am compelled by God to do it. How terrible for me if I didn't preach the Good News!

Paul presented why he was not taking support from others even though it was his right to do so. He thought it was important to be able to say he was not receiving support for his preaching. On the other hand, he knew he could not boast about this because he was compelled by God to do it.

REFLECT

Has God given you a strong feeling that you are to do something without expecting a financial response, even as Paul did?

RESPOND

Talk with a friend about Proverbs 11:24–25. Visit about the times you have been refreshed by helping someone without expecting anything in return.

RECEIVE

DAY 4

1 Corinthians 9:17-18

[17] If I were doing this on my own initiative, I would deserve payment. But I have no choice, for God has given me this sacred trust. [18] What then is my pay? It is the opportunity to preach the Good News without charging anyone. That's why I never demand my rights when I preach the Good News.

Paul was not receiving support for faithfully preaching the gospel. His riches were spiritual instead of material. Even though this was his choice as an apostle, it does not mean others must do the same. Paul worked to support himself as he preached to others without charge. Today that is often called a "bi-vocational" ministry.

REFLECT

Are you teaching others about the Scriptures without charge? If so, you can be spiritually rich even if not materially rich.

RESPOND

For Paul's skill in supporting himself, read Acts 18:1-3. Do you know of others who have a bi-vocational ministry?

RECEIVE

1 Corinthians 9:19-20

[19] Even though I am a free man with no master, I have become a slave to all people to bring many to Christ. [20] When I was with the Jews, I lived like a Jew to bring the Jews to Christ. When I was with those who follow the Jewish law, I too lived under that law. Even though I am not subject to the law, I did this so I could bring to Christ those who are under the law.

This is a passage commonly misunderstood. Some think that in order to evangelize others Paul broadened out what he would normally do. It seems to be the opposite. He had complete freedom in the grace that Christ had offered. Instead, he gladly limited himself so as not to offend those he was trying to reach with the gospel.

REFLECT

Have you sometimes limited your liberty around those you did not want to offend as you were seeking to win them to Jesus?

RESPOND

It is important to remember that the topic being treated in 1 Corinthians refers to relating to a person who is a "weak" believer. Such a believer is one who has not been properly taught about his liberty in Jesus. It is not about one who has been saved and has studied the Scriptures for years but is acting like a weak believer.

WEEK 20:
1 CORINTHIANS 9, 10

RECEIVE

1 Corinthians 9:21

[21] When I am with the Gentiles who do not follow the Jewish law, I too live apart from that law so I can bring them to Christ. But I do not ignore the law of God; I obey the law of Christ.

Some might take this to mean when they are with those who do not have good moral standards, they can win them to Christ by acting like them. Not so with the apostle Paul. While he witnessed to them who live without law he realized he should "obey the law of Christ." Paul never compromised what he believed about the resurrected Christ. He could adjust to cultural differences but not to false teaching.

REFLECT

As a believer in Jesus, do you refuse to compromise on what the Scriptures teach about Him?

RESPOND

Talk with a friend about what Paul referred to as the "law of Christ." He also used this expression when he wrote Galatians 6:1-3. Think also of the command Jesus gave to believers to love others as He had loved them (see John 13:34).

DAY 2

RECEIVE

1 Corinthians 9:22–23

[22] When I am with those who are weak, I share their weakness, for I want to bring the weak to Christ. Yes, I try to find common ground with everyone, doing everything I can to save some. [23] I do everything to spread the Good News and share in its blessings.

Although he was an apostle of the Lord Jesus Christ, Paul sought to find common ground with everyone. He did not consider himself to be above others. In his endeavor to be an effective witness for Jesus he did all he could to identify with those who needed Jesus.

REFLECT

Do you pray for those the Lord may want you to minister to in a special way? Ask the Lord to burden your heart for someone in special need. Then be faithful in responding.

RESPOND

It is almost impossible to have an effective Christian witness without a relationship. See what Paul wrote in Romans 12:15-16. Practicing this will help you to establish a relationship with your listener and hopefully give you opportunity to share your faith.

RECEIVE

1 Corinthians 9:24-25

²⁴ Don't you realize that in a race everyone runs, but only one person gets the prize? So run to win! ²⁵ All athletes are disciplined in their training. They do it to win a prize that will fade away, but we do it for an eternal prize.

Paul was referring to the athletic games in that day in which only one person won the prize. The Corinthians would be acquainted with those games. He alluded to the discipline athletes needed to have as he made a parallel to the service of a Christian. The athlete did it to attain a crown with a wreath of flowers that would perish. The believer in Jesus disciplines his life to serve Jesus so that he will receive an eternal prize.

REFLECT

Think of your service for Jesus as winning an eternal prize. That perspective makes a difference in the way you serve Him.

RESPOND

For the rewarding of believers for their service, read 1 Corinthians 3:9-15. The one without something worthy of reward does not lose salvation but only the reward. Discuss this passage with a friend as you think about eternal rewards.

RECEIVE

1 Corinthians 9:26–27

²⁶ So I run with purpose in every step. I am not just shadowboxing. ²⁷ I discipline my body like an athlete, training it to do what it should. Otherwise, I fear that after preaching to others I myself might be disqualified.

Paul explained that he was running the Christian race with the discipline that an athlete would exercise for his games. Paul mentioned disciplining his body. Those who do not discipline their bodies are in danger of being set aside because they become unapproved as an effective witness. They don't lose their salvation if they have trusted in Jesus for salvation, only the possibility of their rewards.

REFLECT

Does this passage give you a better perspective on how to live the Christian life? You need to use your mind, emotions, and will as you seek to be an effective witness for Jesus.

RESPOND

Visit with a friend about the concern of not being disqualified in being an effective witness for Jesus. Read 2 Corinthians 13:5–6 to see what Paul wrote in his second letter to the Corinthian church.

DAY 5

RECEIVE

1 Corinthians 10:1-2

[1] I don't want you to forget, dear brothers and sisters, about our ancestors in the wilderness long ago. All of them were guided by a cloud that moved ahead of them, and all of them walked through the sea on dry ground. [2] In the cloud and in the sea, all of them were baptized as followers of Moses.

Paul used the nation Israel as an example for present-day believers. As they crossed the Red Sea they were "baptized as followers of Moses." This reveals that the basic meaning of "baptize" is neither sprinkling nor immersion. They did not get a drop of water on them. The basic meaning of "baptize" is being identified with a person. In this case, it was with Moses.

REFLECT

Have you previously thought about the expression "baptized as followers of Moses"? Is the explanation of help to you?

RESPOND

Discuss with a fellow believer the significance of baptism in being identified with Jesus. Read 1 Corinthians 12:12-13 that records the meaning of Christian baptism.

WEEK 21:
1 CORINTHIANS 10

RECEIVE

1 Corinthians 10:3-5

³ All of them ate the same spiritual food, ⁴ and all of them drank the same spiritual water. For they drank from the spiritual rock that traveled with them, and that rock was Christ. ⁵ Yet God was not pleased with most of them, and their bodies were scattered in the wilderness.

Paul wrote about Israel's experience in the desert. The "spiritual food" was the manna from which "all" benefitted. The "spiritual water" was what God provided from the rock and at other times, from which all benefitted. Paul said that rock prefigured the Lord Jesus Christ. In spite of these miracles "most of them" perished in the wilderness because God was not pleased with them.

REFLECT

Does it concern you about benefitting from the promises of God and yet not pleasing Him?

RESPOND

With a friend read Exodus 16:1-5 that tells about the manna. Also read Exodus 17:1-6 that tells about water from the rock. For another time with water from the rock, read Numbers 20:6-12. Discuss why Moses and Aaron were not allowed to enter the Promised Land.

DAY 2

RECEIVE

1 Corinthians 10:6-8

[6] These things happened as a warning to us, so that we would not crave evil things as they did, [7] or worship idols as some of them did. As the Scriptures say, "The people celebrated with feasting and drinking, and they indulged in pagan revelry." [8] And we must not engage in sexual immorality as some of them did, causing 23,000 of them to die in one day.

Paul wanted the believers in Corinth to realize that what occurred to the Israelites should serve as an example for them. When God calls believers to Himself, He wants them to be sanctified; that is, set apart from the world unto Him. This passage also reveals that actions have consequences. Paul said this should serve as a warning to his readers.

REFLECT

Give serious thought to the fact that your actions result in consequences. This is true for both your good actions as well as your bad ones.

RESPOND

Discuss with another believer how you are set apart from the world to serve and please God. Read Romans 12:1-2 to aid in your discussion.

RECEIVE

DAY 3

1 Corinthians 10:9-11

⁹ Nor should we put Christ to the test, as some of them did and then died from snakebites. ¹⁰ And don't grumble as some of them did, and then were destroyed by the angel of death. ¹¹ These things happened to them as examples for us. They were written down to warn us who live at the end of the age.

Paul continued with what happened to the Israelites that should be an example to present-day readers. He also urged them not to grumble. It seems that one could write across the book of Numbers, "God hates grumbling." The Israelites seemed to never learn that lesson. Paul knew believers in the Body of Christ also needed to learn that lesson.

REFLECT

Have you learned not to grumble at circumstances and instead do as 1 Thessalonians 5:18 commands? You can learn this by believing Romans 8:28.

RESPOND

In 1 Corinthians 10:9-10 Paul referred to two incidents found in Numbers 21:4-9 and Exodus 12:22-23. Read these passages with a friend to learn more about what the apostle Paul was referring to.

RECEIVE

1 Corinthians 10:12-13

[12] If you think you are standing strong, be careful not to fall. [13] The temptations in your life are no different from what others experience. And God is faithful. He will not allow the temptation to be more than you can stand. When you are tempted, he will show you a way out so that you can endure.

Paul had been writing about weak Christians. Here he warns those who think they are strong to be careful not to fall. Some think that the temptation they face is different than what others have faced. Not so, says Paul. Notice that God does not necessarily remove the temptation but shows a way one can endure it.

REFLECT

Are you facing a trial now that you are praying about? Ask the Lord to lessen its intensity that you may be able to bear up under it. The Lord has promised to do that.

RESPOND

With a friend read Romans 5:2-4 as you discuss trials. Talk about what the trials help to produce in your life. Ask God to do this for you.

RECEIVE

DAY 5

1 Corinthians 10:14-16

[14] So, my dear friends, flee from the worship of idols. [15] You are reasonable people. Decide for yourselves if what I am saying is true. [16] When we bless the cup at the Lord's Table, aren't we sharing in the blood of Christ? And when we break the bread, aren't we sharing in the body of Christ?

Paul returned to treating the problem about idols. He wants believers to flee from them. Paul then begins to write about the Lord's Table, or what is commonly called "The Lord's Supper." What was in the cup symbolized the Lord's blood; the broken bread symbolized His broken body. Believers in Jesus share in the Lord's Supper and in this way remember the benefits of what Jesus has done for them.

REFLECT

As a believer, do you look forward to the time at the Lord's Table?

RESPOND

Talk with a friend about the name of the communion service. It is called "The Lord's Table" or "The Lord's Supper." It is not said to be the table of a particular church or denomination. Look forward to more details about this in 1 Corinthians 11.

WEEK 22:
1 CORINTHIANS 10

RECEIVE

DAY 1

1 Corinthians 10:17-18

17 And though we are many, we all eat from one loaf of bread, showing that we are one body. 18 Think about the people of Israel. Weren't they united by eating the sacrifices at the altar?

Just as the Israelites showed their commonality by eating the sacrifices at the altar, believers in Jesus do this at the Lord's Table. Believers today are brothers and sisters in the body of Christ and display this at the Lord's Table.

REFLECT

As you participate in the Lord's Supper, do you feel a deeper bond with fellow believers?

RESPOND

Join with a believer in praying for other believers and ministries that are close to your heart. Pray for one another's family.

RECEIVE

1 Corinthians 10:19-20

[19] What am I trying to say? Am I saying that food offered to idols has some significance, or that idols are real gods? [20] No, not at all. I am saying that these sacrifices are offered to demons, not to God. And I don't want you to participate with demons.

Paul wanted to be understood in what he was saying. He wanted all believers in Jesus to understand that sacrifices to idols were actually being offered to demons. Paul did not want Christ followers to have anything to do with worshiping demons.

REFLECT

Is it your desire to stay as far away as you can from anything connected with the demonic world?

RESPOND

With a friend, read Deuteronomy 18:9-12 to see what Moses told the Israelites. He wanted them to obey his instructions as they entered the Promised Land.

RECEIVE

1 Corinthians 10:21-22

²¹ You cannot drink from the cup of the Lord and from the cup of demons, too. You cannot eat at the Lord's Table and at the table of demons, too. ²² What? Do we dare to rouse the Lord's jealousy? Do you think we are stronger than he is?

The Corinthian believers were living where there was much idol worship. Paul did not want those believers to have anything to do with that culture. Believers should not participate in the Lord's Table and think they could have any part in the table of demons. There would be consequences if they sought to do that.

REFLECT

Do you have a reverential fear of the Lord? You should not raise His jealousy by having anything to do with the demonic world.

RESPOND

Read Deuteronomy 4:15-20 to see God's warning about idolatry. An idol is something that is seen, in contrast to God, who is not seen. In the western world it could be materialism. Matthew 6:24 says one cannot serve two masters.

RECEIVE

DAY 4

1 Corinthians 10:23-24

²³ You say, "I am allowed to do anything"—but not everything is good for you. You say, "I am allowed to do anything"—but not everything is beneficial. ²⁴ Don't be concerned for your own good but for the good of others.

Paul cautioned those who were taking their Christian liberty as a license to disrespect others. It is selfish wanting only to please one's self rather than having the desire to honor Christ in all one does. It is also selfish to be concerned only about yourself and not the good of others.

REFLECT

As you seek to honor the Lord Jesus, are you concerned about how others view your life?

RESPOND

Talk about this with a friend. In thinking about others see Ephesians 5:15-20 that tells how a believer should live.

RECEIVE

DAY 5

1 Corinthians 10:25-27

²⁵ So you may eat any meat that is sold in the marketplace without raising questions of conscience. ²⁶ For "the earth is the Lord's, and everything in it." ²⁷ If someone who isn't a believer asks you home for dinner, accept the invitation if you want to. Eat whatever is offered to you without raising questions of conscience.

It is not necessary for Christians to ask in the marketplace whether something has been offered to an idol. The same is true if the believer is invited to the home of an unbeliever. The Christian should not make something an issue if the host has not.

REFLECT

Does this help you in living the Christian life in front of others? Your main desire should be to live a good testimony before them.

RESPOND

Consider Jesus to be your model of what a Christ follower should be like. The apostle Paul described this in Philippians 2:1-11. Talk about this passage with a friend.

WEEK 23:
1 CORINTHIANS 10, 11

RECEIVE

1 Corinthians 10:28-30

[28] (But suppose someone tells you, "This meat was offered to an idol." Don't eat it, out of consideration for the conscience of the one who told you. [29] It might not be a matter of conscience for you, but it is for the other person.) For why should my freedom be limited by what someone else thinks? [30] If I can thank God for the food and enjoy it, why should I be condemned for eating it?

Paul revealed that a Christian may have liberty and his conscience is not bothered by doing something. But if another person raises an issue, then the believer should take that into consideration. He then treated the problem of selfish Christians even today who do not care what others think.

REFLECT

Are you concerned about what others think? The topic is not about those who have been believers for a long time and are untaught, but about new believers who have not been properly taught.

RESPOND

The problem faced in Paul's day was circumcision. See what he said in Galatians 5:1-3 about this. Today it can be other things that New Testament believers are thinking they need to live by Old Testament regulations. The moral law always applies, but not the Levitical regulations.

RECEIVE

DAY 2

1 Corinthians 10:31-33

[31] So whether you eat or drink, or whatever you do, do it all for the glory of God. [32] Don't give offense to Jews or Gentiles or the church of God. [33] I, too, try to please everyone in everything I do. I don't just do what is best for me; I do what is best for others so that many may be saved.

This is the test for the Christ follower. Can the act under consideration be done for the "glory of God"? Paul was concerned about not offending anyone in three different groups: Jews, Gentiles (unsaved ones), and the church of God (believers in Jesus). There are some today who think that the Church replaced Israel so for them there would be only two groups. That is not what the apostle Paul taught. Notice also the reason why Paul acted as he did.

REFLECT

Do you try to live for the best of others as Paul did? Paul's reason was so they might be saved. Is that also your reason?

RESPOND

Visit with a friend about unsaved friends you both have. Talk and pray about how you can build a better relationship with them. They need to see your life and give you an opportunity to talk about Jesus. Have you asked to share a meal with them?

RECEIVE

DAY 3

1 Corinthians 11:1-3

¹ And you should imitate me, just as I imitate Christ. ² I am so glad that you always keep me in your thoughts, and that you are following the teachings I passed on to you. ³ But there is one thing I want you to know: The head of every man is Christ, the head of woman is man, and the head of Christ is God.

It must be remembered that chapter and verse divisions were not in the original manuscripts. They were added later; chapters around A.D. 1227 and verses around 1555. This is a case where 1 Corinthians 11:1 is thought better to have been at the end of chapter 10. Then 1 Corinthians 11:2 proceeds with a new topic.

REFLECT

Even though translators and others have inserted helpful notes into the text to make it easier for reference, the text itself is what has been inspired by God. You need not have any doubts about that.

RESPOND

This would be a good time with a friend to examine two passages of Scripture that are main ones about the inspiration of the Scripture. See 2 Timothy 3:16-17 and 2 Peter 1:20-21. Do you see how these chapter and verse divisions make it easier to find something?

RECEIVE

1 Corinthians 11:4-5

[4] A man dishonors his head if he covers his head while praying or prophesying. [5] But a woman dishonors her head if she prays or prophesies without a covering on her head, for this is the same as shaving her head.

In 1 Corinthians 11:3 Paul said the head of the man is Christ and the head of the woman is the man. This meaning carries over to verses 4-5. If a man covers his head while praying or prophesying he dishonors Christ. If a woman does not cover her head while she prays or prophesies she dishonors the man. It is generally agreed that these instructions have to do with a married couple.

REFLECT

Have you thought of these verses in this way before? This seems to be what they are saying in this context.

RESPOND

Talk with a friend about how to handle Bible verses whose meaning are debated by others. This problem carries over to the next verse that has been strongly debated.

RECEIVE

DAY 5

1 Corinthians 11:6

⁶ Yes, if she refuses to wear a head covering, she should cut off all her hair! But since it is shameful for a woman to have her hair cut or her head shaved, she should wear a covering.

Some believe the reference to having a shaved head had to do with what the prostitutes were like in the pagan temple in Corinth. Others take the instructions here to apply always. Some church groups teach women should wear hats; other church groups do not. There is no definition about what the hats should look like or how much they should cover.

REFLECT

Are you able to live at peace with believers who differ on this issue?

RESPOND

The apostle Paul wrote much about exercising love toward others. This is one of those matters where Christ followers have been strongly divided. Sometimes believers express more love to unbelievers than they do to fellow believers with whom they disagree. Ephesians 4:32 can also apply here.

WEEK 24:
1 CORINTHIANS 11

RECEIVE

1 Corinthians 11:7-8

7 A man should not wear anything on his head when worshiping, for man is made in God's image and reflects God's glory. And woman reflects man's glory. 8 For the first man didn't come from woman, but the first woman came from man.

There is no reason to debate this passage because of its clarity. Man reflects God's glory and the woman reflects man's glory. The only debate would come from those who believe in evolution instead of creation. This means also those who disagree would need to deny the creation account in Genesis is the true word of God. That is a far bigger problem than the issue in this passage.

REFLECT

Whether you are male or female, do you realize this passage applies to you?

RESPOND

Take the time with a friend to read the accounts in Genesis that tell of the creation of the man and woman. See Genesis 1:26-27 and Genesis 2:21-23. It is considered that Genesis 2 gives more details about the creation account in Genesis 1.

RECEIVE

1 Corinthians 11:9-10

⁹ And man was not made for woman, but woman was made for man. ¹⁰ For this reason, and because the angels are watching, a woman should wear a covering on her head to show she is under authority.

Paul referred to the angels watching mankind. There are questions about whether those in heaven now are watching those yet living on earth. The Bible is not clear on that. But it is clear that the angels watch those on earth. Paul indicated the woman wearing a sign of authority on her head was a witness to the angels.

REFLECT

Is it a new concept to you to realize the angels are watching you?

RESPOND

Talk with a friend about the current ministry of angels. See Hebrews 1:6, 7, 14. Some speak of loved ones being taken to heaven by angels. Luke 16:22 indicates angels carried the poor man to Abraham's side, likely another name for heaven.

RECEIVE

1 Corinthians 11:11-12

¹¹ But among the Lord's people, women are not independent of men, and men are not independent of women. ¹² For although the first woman came from man, every other man was born from a woman, and everything comes from God.

Paul revealed how both men and women are dependent on one another. The first woman came from Adam but all men since then have come from women. Paul added that "everything comes from God." It is God's plan. No man should think he is independent from a woman, and no woman should think she is independent from a man.

REFLECT

Do you recognize that your gender is in the plan of God?

RESPOND

Talk with a friend about the idea being propagated in the world that there are more than two genders. Such thinking disregards what God has done. Those espousing such false views are setting themselves up as God to decide what is right and wrong. Read Romans 1:18-32 to see what God does to such people and allows them to do.

RECEIVE

DAY 4

1 Corinthians 11:13-14

[13] Judge for yourselves. Is it right for a woman to pray to God in public without covering her head? [14] Isn't it obvious that it's disgraceful for a man to have long hair?

Paul returns to talking about the custom of his day. Even verse 14 has caused debate. How long is long? There seems to be a basic principle that men should not try to look like women, and women should not try to look like men.

REFLECT

Do you seek to look like your gender? In what ways do you do this?

RESPOND

With a friend read 1 Timothy 2:9-10. In this passage Paul instructed Timothy, a pastor, how women should adorn themselves for worship. He appealed for inner beauty and attracting others by their good works.

RECEIVE

DAY 5

1 Corinthians 11:15-16

[15] And isn't long hair a woman's pride and joy? For it has been given to her as a covering. [16] But if anyone wants to argue about this, I simply say that we have no other custom than this, and neither do God's other churches.

Most would agree that a woman's hair is her pride and joy. It has been said of women in nursing homes that when a woman does not want her hair fixed, she is in serious decline. Paul refused to argue about this custom and said it was the only one in the other churches.

REFLECT

Is this an important issue in the church you attend? Do people express their differences with love?

RESPOND

Paul is building toward 1 Corinthians 13, which is the great love chapter in the Bible. Regardless of how believers think about a problem, if it is not some doctrinal issue that has to do with eternal life, the topic should be handled with love while seeking to understand the other person's thoughts.

WEEK 25:
1 CORINTHIANS 11

RECEIVE

1 Corinthians 11:17-19

[17] But in the following instructions, I cannot praise you. For it sounds as if more harm than good is done when you meet together. [18] First, I hear that there are divisions among you when you meet as a church, and to some extent I believe it. [19] But, of course, there must be divisions among you so that you who have God's approval will be recognized!

Paul could not praise the Corinthians about a report he had heard. He was disappointed with the lack of harmony among those in the church fellowship. He realized that divisions in a church have a good purpose: they reveal who is approved by God. This is something most churches today do not think about.

REFLECT

Have you had cliques in the church you attend? What was the result of them? Were people hurt spiritually?

RESPOND

With a friend talk about what divisions can do in a church. Read 1 John 2:18-19 to help in your discussion.

RECEIVE

1 Corinthians 11:20-21

[20] When you meet together, you are not really interested in the Lord's Supper. [21] For some of you hurry to eat your own meal without sharing with others. As a result, some go hungry while others get drunk.

Paul chided the church goers who came to celebrate the Lord's Supper. Normally a fellowship meal called a "love feast" preceded participating in the Lord's Supper. Apparently the more affluent were not sharing with the poorer people. The wealthier hurried to eat the meal before the poorer people arrived. Some had even drunk so much wine at the love feast that they were drunk by the time it came to participate in the Lord's Supper.

REFLECT

Does your church group have a fellowship meal before the Lord's Supper? Some do.

RESPOND

What do you and your friend do so you are not separated from those less fortunate? Have you asked the less fortunate to your home for a meal? That can provide an opportunity to talk about spiritual matters and enable you to share your faith with others.

RECEIVE

DAY 3

1 Corinthians 11:22

²² What? Don't you have your own homes for eating and drinking? Or do you really want to disgrace God's church and shame the poor? What am I supposed to say? Do you want me to praise you? Well, I certainly will not praise you for this!

To those who were not expressing love at the love feast, Paul asked if they did not have homes for eating and drinking. What they were doing, Paul said, was disgracing God's church. It was also degrading the poor. The guilty ones may have expected Paul to praise them but he refused to do so because of their behavior.

REFLECT

How do you think the readers felt who were guilty of these actions?

RESPOND

With a friend read Jude 1:12-13 about ungodly people eating with others at the love feasts. Christ followers need to be on guard about those in their midst who are not true believers in Jesus.

RECEIVE

DAY 4

1 Corinthians 11:23–24

²³ For I pass on to you what I received from the Lord himself. On the night when he was betrayed, the Lord Jesus took some bread ²⁴ and gave thanks to God for it. Then he broke it in pieces and said, "This is my body, which is given for you. Do this in remembrance of me."

Paul expressed what he had received by revelation from the Lord. This is what Jesus said on the night He was betrayed. At the meal, He picked up the bread, broke it in pieces and said it was a symbol of His body which was given for believers. It was to be eaten and in this way remembering what He had done for them.

REFLECT

How often does your church fellowship celebrate the Lord's Supper? What are the reasons for this?

RESPOND

Consider how sobering it is during the Lord's Supper to realize the broken bread is a symbol of Jesus' broken body for lost mankind. Thinking on this should humble every Christ follower.

RECEIVE

1 Corinthians 11:25-26

²⁵ In the same way, he took the cup of wine after supper, saying, "This cup is the new covenant between God and his people—an agreement confirmed with my blood. Do this in remembrance of me as often as you drink it." ²⁶ For every time you eat this bread and drink this cup, you are announcing the Lord's death until he comes again.

Jesus' action after breaking the bread was followed by what he said about the contents of the cup. It was the "new covenant between God and his people." That covenant was confirmed by His blood. The Bible does not specify a specific time or the number of times the Lord's Supper is to be observed. Jesus simply said, "as often as you drink it." Eating the bread and drinking the cup announces the Lord's death until His Second Advent to earth.

REFLECT

Have you heard people debate how often the Lord's Supper should be observed? Does anyone point out what the Bible says?

RESPOND

Join with a friend in reading the new covenant to which Jesus referred. It is found in Jeremiah 31:31-34. See also what is said about it in Hebrews 8:6-13.

WEEK 26:
1 CORINTHIANS 11, 12

RECEIVE

1 Corinthians 11:27-28

[27] So anyone who eats this bread or drinks this cup of the Lord unworthily is guilty of sinning against the body and blood of the Lord. [28] That is why you should examine yourself before eating the bread and drinking the cup.

No one is worthy of what Jesus has done for lost mankind. The unworthy manner that the Corinthians were displaying had to do with the love feast where they were not showing love to others. All believers are in the body of Christ, the Church. Paul urged believers to examine themselves to be sure there is no sin that needs to be confessed or made right with others.

REFLECT

When your church group participates in the Lord's Supper, does it give time for believers to quietly examine themselves?

RESPOND

Notice with a friend how Jesus feels when believers in His body are attacked. Unbelieving Saul was on the road to Damascus for the purpose of persecuting Christians. Jesus appeared to him and asked, "Why are you persecuting me?" (see Acts 9:4). Jesus considered anyone persecuting Christ followers are actually persecuting Him.

DAY 2

RECEIVE

1 Corinthians 11:29-30

²⁹ For if you eat the bread or drink the cup without honoring the body of Christ, you are eating and drinking God's judgment upon yourself. ³⁰ That is why many of you are weak and sick and some have even died.

Paul gave a serious warning to the Corinthian church. The group was acting in an unworthy manner as it had a love feast followed by the Lord's Supper. Some had a bad attitude toward fellow believers and God had disciplined them. As a result, some were weak and sick and some had died. This does not mean they lost their eternal salvation but they lost their physical life.

REFLECT

Do you understand that sometimes God disciplines His children?

RESPOND

With a friend read Hebrews 12:5-11. This passage tells how God sometimes deals with His spiritual children.

RECEIVE

DAY 3

1 Corinthians 11:31-32

[31] But if we would examine ourselves, we would not be judged by God in this way. [32] Yet when we are judged by the Lord, we are being disciplined so that we will not be condemned along with the world.

Paul instructed believers to examine themselves so God would not have to discipline them. This assumes any sin would be confessed and made right with anyone who had been offended. When the heart is made right, then one is qualified to participate in the Lord's Supper.

REFLECT

Have you experienced having to deal with an issue in your heart before taking the Lord's Supper?

RESPOND

Join with a friend in reading 2 Corinthians 13:5. This passage tells of the need to determine whether one is in the faith. Talk with your friend about how each of you has assurance of your salvation.

RECEIVE

DAY 4

1 Corinthians 11:33–34

[33] So, my dear brothers and sisters, when you gather for the Lord's Supper, wait for each other. [34] If you are really hungry, eat at home so you won't bring judgment upon yourselves when you meet together. I'll give you instructions about the other matters after I arrive.

Paul gave his final instructions about how the love feast should be handled before the people participated in the Lord's Supper. He did not want them to bring God's judgment on themselves. There were other things that needed to be commented on, but Paul assured them he would address those when he visited them.

REFLECT

Have Paul's instructions about observing the Lord's Supper been helpful to you? What have you had emphasized in your mind about his instructions?

RESPOND

Take the time with a friend to reread 1 Corinthians 11:17–34. Talk about what has especially impressed each of you about Paul's instructions.

DAY 5

RECEIVE

1 Corinthians 12:1-3

[1] Now, dear brothers and sisters, regarding your question about the special abilities the Spirit gives us. I don't want you to misunderstand this. [2] You know that when you were still pagans, you were led astray and swept along in worshiping speechless idols. [3] So I want you to know that no one speaking by the Spirit of God will curse Jesus, and no one can say Jesus is Lord, except by the Holy Spirit.

Paul turned his attention to answering another question the Corinthian believers had asked. It had to do with special gifts the Holy Spirit gives to believers. Paul reminded them that when they were without Jesus they worshiped idols that couldn't talk. Now they seemed to be especially concerned about what talk was of the Spirit and what was not.

REFLECT

This begins an important topic in the New Testament. It is worth your careful attention.

RESPOND

In preparation for 1 Corinthians 12, talk with your friend about spiritual gifts. As you discuss the topic it will increase your desire to know what the apostle Paul said about spiritual gifts in 1 Corinthians 12. It is a topic that will extend through 1 Corinthians 14.

Week 27:
1 Corinthians 12

RECEIVE

1 Corinthians 12:4-6

[4] There are different kinds of spiritual gifts, but the same Spirit is the source of them all. [5] There are different kinds of service, but we serve the same Lord. [6] God works in different ways, but it is the same God who does the work in all of us.

Notice the mention of the three persons of the Godhead in this verse—the Spirit, Lord, and God. Although there are various kinds of gifts, it is the same God distributing them. Those gifts are given to people who will use them to help the body of Christ and honor God.

REFLECT

Consider that the various gifts have the same source. They are intended to be different ways of serving and honoring the Lord by helping fellow believers.

RESPOND

With a friend, read other portions of Scripture that talk about spiritual gifts. Together read Romans 12:6-8; Ephesians 4:7-13; and 1 Peter 4:10-11. These passages will give you more understanding about spiritual gifts and gifted people.

RECEIVE

DAY 2

1 Corinthians 12:7

[7] A spiritual gift is given to each of us so we can help each other.

This verse needs extra consideration. There are many believers in Jesus who do not think they have been gifted to do anything. Yet, this verse says a spiritual gift "is given to each of us." No believer is excluded in this statement. Notice also why the gift is given: "so we can help each other." The gift is not for you to use for your glory but to use to help others in the body of Christ.

REFLECT

As a believer, think about what spiritual gift you have been given. How are you using it to help others?

RESPOND

Visit with a Christian friend and discuss what spiritual gift each of you think you have. Sometimes it is discovered by helping spiritually with whatever you can. Then you may find one thing you do is especially helpful to fellow Christians. That may be your gift.

RECEIVE

DAY 3

1 Corinthians 12:8–9

[8] To one person the Spirit gives the ability to give wise advice; to another the same Spirit gives a message of special knowledge. [9] The same Spirit gives great faith to another, and to someone else the one Spirit gives the gift of healing.

The emphasis in this passage is that the various gifts come from the same Holy Spirit. Although the gifts have to do with "wise advice"; "special knowledge"; and "the gift of healing"; they are each given to a believer by the same Spirit. It seems the Corinthians were divided about which gift was the best and Paul was reminding them that all spiritual gifts came from the same Spirit.

REFLECT

Are you sensitive to the fact that whatever spiritual gift you have it has been given by the Holy Spirit? This means He should get the praise for what you are enabled to do.

RESPOND

Spend time with a friend thanking God for the ministry He has given each of you. Pray for the friends you have been able to encourage spiritually.

RECEIVE

1 Corinthians 12:10-11

[10] He gives one person the power to perform miracles, and another the ability to prophesy. He gives someone else the ability to discern whether a message is from the Spirit of God or from another spirit. Still another person is given the ability to speak in unknown languages, while another is given the ability to interpret what is being said. [11] It is the one and only Spirit who distributes all these gifts. He alone decides which gift each person should have.

Paul lists more gifts the Holy Spirit gives. One must remember that Paul was writing this about A.D. 55 before the Scriptures were completed as they are today. "Prophecy" in that day included both "forth telling" and "foretelling." That is, it had to do with giving out God's message before the Scriptures were completed. Sometimes it included future predictions. The "unknown languages" were languages not known to the speaker but were known at that time in the world.

REFLECT

If you have questions about some of these gifts, you should visit with your pastor.

RESPOND

The book of Jude has only one chapter. See verse 3 about Jude's statement that he was writing about the faith God had given His people "once and for all time." This indicates that nothing needs to be added to the Scriptures available today.

RECEIVE

1 Corinthians 12:12-13

¹² The human body has many parts, but the many parts make up one whole body. So it is with the body of Christ. ¹³ Some of us are Jews, some are Gentiles, some are slaves, and some are free. But we have all been baptized into one body by one Spirit, and we all share the same Spirit.

This is an important verse explaining what "baptism" refers to. It is mentioned other times in the Scriptures but this passage reveals it has to do with being placed into the body of Christ at the time one believes in Jesus as Savior. Regardless of one's nationality or ethnic group, all are placed into the same body of Christ known as the universal Church.

REFLECT

Thank the Lord that others from different backgrounds are in the same body of Christ you are if they have believed in Him as Savior. The universal Church includes believers from all over the world. A local church is what you hopefully are part of with fellow believers.

RESPOND

The basic meaning of baptism has to do with identification. See 1 Corinthians 10:2 to see the Israelites were "baptized" as followers of Moses. They did not get any water on them; they were identified with him. After trusting in Jesus as Savior, believers are baptized to show their identification with Him and His followers.

WEEK 28:
1 CORINTHIANS 12

RECEIVE

1 Corinthians 12:14-17

¹⁴ Yes, the body has many different parts, not just one part.
¹⁵ If the foot says, "I am not a part of the body because I am not a hand," that does not make it any less a part of the body.
¹⁶ And if the ear says, "I am not part of the body because I am not an eye," would that make it any less a part of the body?
¹⁷ If the whole body were an eye, how would you hear? Or if your whole body were an ear, how would you smell anything?

Apparently some of the Corinthian believers thought their particular gift was what everyone should have. Paul tells them all the different gifts are necessary for the body of Christ to properly function. His parallel to the human body was to help them see how all the parts of it are necessary. They needed to receive what Paul was saying about this.

REFLECT

Have you been helped to see that God needs all the spiritual gifts working through His people for His Church to be functioning properly?

RESPOND

With your friend read Hebrews 10:25. Notice that "assembling" is more than just being there. Parts of a machine can be in the same building but not assembled. There needs to be a functioning together.

DAY 2

RECEIVE

1 Corinthians 12:18–21

[18] But our bodies have many parts, and God has put each part just where he wants it. [19] How strange a body would be if it had only one part! [20] Yes, there are many parts, but only one body. [21] The eye can never say to the hand, "I don't need you." The head can't say to the feet, "I don't need you."

Paul draws on the analogy of the human body to show that all parts are needed. So also it is with spiritual gifts in the Church. The Corinthians were likely magnifying one gift and minimizing others. Paul was showing them that all parts are needed.

REFLECT

Do you recognize how the spiritual gifts of others are needed along with your gift?

RESPOND

Read 2 Corinthians 13:11 to see how Paul closed his second letter to them. He tells believers how to live with each other.

RECEIVE

1 Corinthians 12:22-24

²² In fact, some parts of the body that seem weakest and least important are actually the most necessary. ²³ And the parts we regard as less honorable are those we clothe with the greatest care. So we carefully protect those parts that should not be seen, ²⁴ while the more honorable parts do not require this special care. So God has put the body together such that extra honor and care are given to those parts that have less dignity.

Paul stressed that those members of the body that are not thought much about are important. Think of meetings in the church where some members are in the limelight but others are working behind the scenes to make everything work well. Summer camps need a good speaker, but much work is needed in the kitchen and by the ground crews to make the camp successful.

REFLECT

Are you one that works behind the scenes or in the limelight?

RESPOND

No matter what you do, it can be done to the glory of God. Colossians 3:23 is a verse that should guide your life. See John 11:4 to see that even sickness can be to the glory of God. See John 21:19 for the comment of Jesus that Peter would glorify God through his death.

RECEIVE

DAY 4

1 Corinthians 12:25-26

[25] This makes for harmony among the members, so that all the members care for each other. [26] If one part suffers, all the parts suffer with it, and if one part is honored, all the parts are glad.

Think what this is like. If you injure a finger your whole hand likely feels like it hurts. The same with injuring a toe and it feeling like your entire foot is hurting. So also with believers in the body of Christ. If one believer is suffering, other believers are affected. If one is honored, then all believers should feel they have been honored.

REFLECT

When a fellow believer has a heart ache, do you also grieve? When someone is honored, do you rejoice or are you jealous?

RESPOND

With your friend read Romans 12:15. This is the kind of empathy believers should have for each other.

RECEIVE

DAY 5

1 Corinthians 12:27-28

[27] All of you together are Christ's body, and each of you is a part of it. [28] Here are some of the parts God has appointed for the church: first are apostles, second are prophets, third are teachers, then those who do miracles, those who have the gift of healing, those who can help others, those who have the gift of leadership, those who speak in unknown languages.

Paul listed various gifts and gifted people that are in Christ's body, the Church. 1 Corinthians 12-14 deals with spiritual gifts and especially that of speaking in tongues. As Paul listed the gifts in 12:28 that gift was the last on his list. Not all in the list are needed today, such as apostles and prophets, as they were in Bible times before the Bible was completed. Notice that even those who can help others are listed as a gift.

REFLECT

Notice that some of these gifts put a person in the limelight, but others, such as helps, are behind the scenes. Each is important, however.

RESPOND

Visit with a friend about this list of gifts. Talk about how you might fit into this list, and how you see others fitting into it. This list does not seem to be entirely complete as we considered other passages previously, referred to in Romans 12; Ephesians 4; and 1 Peter 4.

WEEK 29:
1 CORINTHIANS 12, 13

RECEIVE

1 Corinthians 12:29-31

[29] Are we all apostles? Are we all prophets? Are we all teachers? Do we all have the power to do miracles? [30] Do we all have the gift of healing? Do we all have the ability to speak in unknown languages? Do we all have the ability to interpret unknown languages? Of course not! [31] So you should earnestly desire the most helpful gifts. But now let me show you a way of life that is best of all.

Apparently some of the Corinthians thought everyone should have the same spiritual gift they had. The apostle Paul shows that was not what God intended. Paul told them to desire the most "helpful gifts." Some were more concerned about focusing on themselves rather than focusing on what could be for the greater good of those in their fellowship. Then he promised to tell them about the best way of life.

REFLECT

How is it in your fellowship group? Are some more concerned about boasting of the spiritual gift they have rather than being concerned about helping the group?

RESPOND

With a friend read 1 Peter 4:11 about the gift of helping others. Most do not boast about having this gift; they just go on their way helping others and using their gift.

RECEIVE

DAY 2

1 Corinthians 13:1

¹ If I could speak all the languages of earth and of angels, but didn't love others, I would only be a noisy gong or a clanging cymbal.

Receive these words from the apostle Paul about how important love is no matter what spiritual gift you have. 1 Corinthians 13 is considered the great love chapter in the Bible. If you don't have love for others it does not matter what gift you are exercising.

REFLECT

This verse needs to sink into the hearts of all believers in Jesus. Has it sunk into yours?

RESPOND

Join with a friend in reading what Jesus said were the two greatest commandments. Jesus was asked by an expert in the Old Testament law trying to trap Him about the greatest commandment. His answer is recorded in Matthew 22:37-40. This coincides with what 1 Corinthians 13:1 is saying.

RECEIVE

DAY 3

1 Corinthians 13:2-3

[2] If I had the gift of prophecy, and if I understood all of God's secret plans and possessed all knowledge, and if I had such faith that I could move mountains, but didn't love others, I would be nothing. [3] If I gave everything I have to the poor and even sacrificed my body, I could boast about it; but if I didn't love others, I would have gained nothing.

Paul continued mentioning various gifts to show their little value if not accompanied with love. Without love for others the believer "would be nothing" and "would have gained nothing." One wonders what the Corinthian believers thought as they read this verse in Paul's letter.

REFLECT

Think of these verses as showing believers would go from being a hero to a zero if they don't exercise love.

RESPOND

Talk with a friend about this passage. It reveals believers without love for others amount to nothing and gain nothing no matter what spiritual gift they exercise. Talk about how this applies to both of you.

RECEIVE

DAY 4

1 Corinthians 13:4-7

4 Love is patient and kind. Love is not jealous or boastful or proud 5 or rude. It does not demand its own way. It is not irritable, and it keeps no record of being wronged. 6 It does not rejoice about injustice but rejoices whenever the truth wins out. 7 Love never gives up, never loses faith, is always hopeful, and endures through every circumstance.

Paul gave the characteristics of love. These relate to some of the problems the Corinthian church was experiencing. This passage is useful for all believers to think about. It can be a measuring stick to help one know whether he or she has expressed love in the biblical way.

REFLECT

Think of your life in the last couple of weeks. Were these characteristics of love seen in your life?

RESPOND

Visit with a friend about the various relationships you have. Talk about how you could do better in expressing these characteristics of love. Read Galatians 5:22-23 to see the fruit of the Spirit. Are these fruit seen in your lives?

DAY 5

RECEIVE

1 Corinthians 13:8-10

[8] Prophecy and speaking in unknown languages and special knowledge will become useless. But love will last forever!
[9] Now our knowledge is partial and incomplete, and even the gift of prophecy reveals only part of the whole picture!
[10] But when the time of perfection comes, these partial things will become useless.

Paul mentioned the gifts that were useful for time but would not be needed in eternity. Love will last forever because God is love (see 1 John 4:16). Time on earth is like a time of immaturity as information is gained, but when maturity (perfection) comes what helped in immaturity will no longer be needed.

REFLECT

When the Scriptures were completed believers have the full revelation of God.

RESPOND

With a friend read Hebrews 2:3-4. It is considered that Hebrews was written shortly before the destruction of Jerusalem in A.D. 70. Notice that the confirming of God's message is spoken of in the past tense. This indicates the signs, wonders, and miracles were not going on by that time.

WEEK 30:
1 CORINTHIANS 13, 14

RECEIVE

1 Corinthians 13:11-12

[11] When I was a child, I spoke and thought and reasoned as a child. But when I grew up, I put away childish things. [12] Now we see things imperfectly, like puzzling reflections in a mirror, but then we will see everything with perfect clarity. All that I know now is partial and incomplete, but then I will know everything completely, just as God now knows me completely.

Some claim some of these gifts will go from Paul's time to eternity. His example of his youth, however, does not indicate a straight line from birth until death. There is youth to adulthood, then a line to that which is perfect or complete. He admitted that what he knew at the time of his writing was partial and incomplete. He looked forward to the time when he would know everything completely as God knew him.

REFLECT

There are many things in this life that are not understood. Do you look forward to the time when you will know everything completely?

RESPOND

When believers think of eternity with Jesus, 1 John 3:2-3 is a great passage to meditate on. The more the truth of these verses is realized, the purer the believer will seek to be in life.

RECEIVE

1 Corinthians 13:13

¹³ Three things will last forever—faith, hope, and love—and the greatest of these is love.

Paul concluded his emphasis on love by reminding the readers that someday faith and hope would not be needed. Love, on the other hand, will be the great characteristic in heaven because God is love (see 1 John 4:7-9). Faith and hope will last but will not be needed in eternity when the reality is experienced. One's growth in love will be even more greatly experienced in heaven.

REFLECT

Consider how wonderful it will be when believers see Jesus face to face. If you have confidence in doing so, use that in your witnessing by telling others you hope it will also be true for them.

RESPOND

Visit with a friend about the difference of the gifts of the Spirit mentioned in 1 Corinthians 12 and the fruit of the Spirit mentioned in Galatians 5:22-23. By emphasizing love, Paul was stressing to the Corinthians the need to have love in what they were doing in expressing their gifts.

RECEIVE

DAY 3

1 Corinthians 14:1-2

[1] Let love be your highest goal! But you should also desire the special abilities the Spirit gives—especially the ability to prophesy. [2] For if you have the ability to speak in tongues, you will be talking only to God, since people won't be able to understand you. You will be speaking by the power of the Spirit, but it will all be mysterious.

Paul returned to the topic of exercising the gifts of the Spirit after he had stressed the importance of love. He wanted them to desire the special abilities the Holy Spirit gives them but they were to express them in love. Before the Bible was written, the ability to prophesy was both speaking forth the truth of God as well as giving some predictions.

REFLECT

Think of how blessed you are now to have God's written word in the Bible. If you wonder what God says, check your Bible.

RESPOND

Visit with a friend about the contrast Paul is beginning to make in this passage. In 1 Corinthians 14:2 he emphasizes that the one speaking in a language he does not understand talks only to God. The following passage will indicate what Paul desired the Corinthians would do.

RECEIVE

1 Corinthians 14:3-4

³ But one who prophesies strengthens others, encourages them, and comforts them. ⁴ A person who speaks in tongues is strengthened personally, but one who speaks a word of prophecy strengthens the entire church.

This reveals the concern of the apostle Paul. He wanted believers to give out God's word plainly so it would encourage and comfort others in the fellowship. The tongues-speaker would strengthen himself or herself; the prophecy-speaker would strengthen all the church members.

REFLECT

Even today, is it your desire to do something that only benefits you, or is it your desire to benefit others?

RESPOND

Talk with a friend about Paul's emphasis on serving others. See Romans 12:6-8 and count the number of times he tells about doing something for others.

RECEIVE

1 Corinthians 14:5

⁵ I wish you could all speak in tongues, but even more I wish you could all prophesy. For prophecy is greater than speaking in tongues, unless someone interprets what you are saying so that the whole church will be strengthened.

Some like to point to this passage and say, "That is what we should tell Christians today." They forget Paul was writing this about A.D. 55 before the Bible had been completed. Even at that time, it was better, Paul said, to use the gift of prophecy that would be understood by others without anyone having to interpret what was said.

REFLECT

Is it your desire to speak plainly to others so what you say does not have to be explained by someone else?

RESPOND

Visit with a friend about the matter of speaking in a language unknown by the speaker and how often it is mentioned in the Bible. It is primarily in the book of Acts where it is only seen in chapters 2 (the beginning of the New Testament Church), 10 (showing that Gentiles were accepted into the Church), 19 (showing the followers of John the Baptist were accepted into the Church), and perhaps in chapter 8 that referred to the Samaritans who were accepted into the Church. As seen in 1 Corinthians 12-14, it is seen only as Paul is attempting to correct some problems with it.

WEEK 31:
1 CORINTHIANS 14

RECEIVE

1 Corinthians 14:6–8

⁶ Dear brothers and sisters, if I should come to you speaking in an unknown language, how would that help you? But if I bring you a revelation or some special knowledge or prophecy or teaching, that will be helpful. ⁷ Even lifeless instruments like the flute or the harp must play the notes clearly, or no one will recognize the melody. ⁸ And if the bugler doesn't sound a clear call, how will the soldiers know they are being called to battle?

Paul explained why a language heard that others do not understand does not benefit them. On the other hand, a message from God told to others in a language they understand does help them. He illustrates his point by referring to lifeless instruments and a bugler if they give uncertain sounds. His entire point is that communication must be understood to be helpful.

REFLECT

Have you experienced being in a group where someone spoke a language others did not understand? Did it help the group?

RESPOND

Join with a friend to pray for those involved today in translating the Bible into the heart language of others. A significant change comes into their lives when they hear or read God's word in their own tongue.

RECEIVE

1 Corinthians 14:9

⁹ It's the same for you. If you speak to people in words they don't understand, how will they know what you are saying? You might as well be talking into empty space.

After giving examples of messages that are not clear, Paul asked a question. He makes the point it is useless to speak in a language others do not understand. He told them they "might as well be talking into empty space." Believers in Jesus realize they need to be understood if they are to clearly give God's message to others.

REFLECT

Whatever language you speak, there are different levels of understanding in it. One should not use scholarly sounding words for a person with limited use of the language.

RESPOND

This reveals that those who minister need to know their target audience. It is not a problem to use theological terms as long as the speaker defines what they mean. Not defining unfamiliar terms will only confuse the listeners.

DAY 3

RECEIVE

1 Corinthians 14:10-12

[10] There are many different languages in the world, and every language has meaning. [11] But if I don't understand a language, I will be a foreigner to someone who speaks it, and the one who speaks it will be a foreigner to me. [12] And the same is true for you. Since you are so eager to have the special abilities the Spirit gives, seek those that will strengthen the whole church.

Paul expressed his burden for the believers in the Corinthian fellowship. He wanted them to desire to build up the group, not just exercise a gift that built up themselves. If they speak with a language even the speaker does not understand, it may give him a good feeling, but it will not be of help to others.

REFLECT

Consider again the apostle's main point: your spiritual gift should be used to help the entire church fellowship.

RESPOND

Join with a friend in reading Ephesians 4:11-13. This passage reveals that God gave gifted people to the church to build it up. Another word commonly used for "build up" is "edify."

RECEIVE

1 Corinthians 14:13-14

[13] So anyone who speaks in tongues should pray also for the ability to interpret what has been said. [14] For if I pray in tongues, my spirit is praying, but I don't understand what I am saying.

Paul pointed out that one's task is not done just by speaking in a language he does not understand. He needs also to pray for himself or someone else to be able to interpret the language he does not understand.

REFLECT

Not all churches agree on this issue of speaking in tongues. For those who practice it, however, do they also pray for someone to interpret the language that was not understood?

RESPOND

Visit with a friend about how to fellowship with those with differing opinions about speaking in tongues. Seek to practice what Paul said about love even if you do not agree.

RECEIVE

DAY 5

1 Corinthians 14:15-17

[15] Well then, what shall I do? I will pray in the spirit, and I will also pray in words I understand. I will sing in the spirit, and I will also sing in words I understand. [16] For if you praise God only in the spirit, how can those who don't understand you praise God along with you? How can they join you in giving thanks when they don't understand what you are saying? [17] You will be giving thanks very well, but it won't strengthen the people who hear you.

Paul gives his conclusion about the matter under consideration. His desire was to both pray and sing with words he understood. Using understandable words in praising God is also necessary so that others can praise and thank God with you. Again, he mentioned about doing that which will benefit the group, not just a single individual.

REFLECT

This is a difficult issue to wrestle with. Hopefully, you are helped by thinking more about it.

RESPOND

Read Romans 14:17-19 that tells about the apostle Paul's desire for believers. Visit with a friend about this and discuss whether the church fellowship you attend is doing this.

WEEK 32:
1 CORINTHIANS 14

RECEIVE

1 Corinthians 14:18-19

¹⁸ I thank God that I speak in tongues more than any of you.
¹⁹ But in a church meeting I would rather speak five understandable words to help others than ten thousand words in an unknown language.

Before the time the Bible was completed Paul was able to say, "I thank God that I speak in tongues more than any of you." But notice he also said, "But in a church meeting I would rather speak five understandable words to help others than ten thousand words in an unknown language." He continued to emphasize the importance of building up the entire group.

REFLECT

May God use you with whatever spiritual gift you have to benefit the entire church.

RESPOND

With a friend consider what Paul said about the "whole church." See 1 Corinthians 14:5, 12. Read also 1 Corinthians 14:19 where he refers to helping others in the church group.

RECEIVE

1 Corinthians 14:20-21

[20] Dear brothers and sisters, don't be childish in your understanding of these things. Be innocent as babies when it comes to evil, but be mature in understanding matters of this kind. [21] It is written in the Scriptures: "I will speak to my own people through strange languages and through the lips of foreigners. But even then, they will not listen to me," says the Lord.

Paul begins to explain to the Corinthians the background of different languages. In the Old Testament the common language was Hebrew. When God wished to discipline His people He would bring against them those who spoke other languages (see Deuteronomy 28:49; Isaiah 28:11; Jeremiah 5:15).

REFLECT

Have you considered the background of how God used other languages (tongues) in the Old Testament?

RESPOND

With a friend examine the Scriptures referred to in Deuteronomy, Isaiah and Jeremiah. This will give you a better understanding for what Paul later writes in 1 Corinthians 14.

RECEIVE

1 Corinthians 14:22-23

²² So you see that speaking in tongues is a sign, not for believers, but for unbelievers. Prophecy, however, is for the benefit of believers, not unbelievers. ²³ Even so, if unbelievers or people who don't understand these things come into your church meeting and hear everyone speaking in an unknown language, they will think you are crazy.

The apostle Paul wrote "speaking in tongues is a sign . . . for unbelievers." Of what were they a sign? This indicated it was a sign of God disciplining or changing His program for the Jews. This is the indication of what occurred in Acts 2. The speaking in tongues indicated God was turning to the Gentiles. Paul gave reasons for not using tongues to reach unbelievers in the local church.

REFLECT

Have you thought before about what speaking in different languages was a sign of?

RESPOND

When discussing the controversial issue of speaking in tongues it is good to talk about the background of them. This helps to know why God used them.

RECEIVE

DAY 4

1 Corinthians 14:24-25

[24] But if all of you are prophesying, and unbelievers or people who don't understand these things come into your meeting, they will be convicted of sin and judged by what you say. [25] As they listen, their secret thoughts will be exposed, and they will fall to their knees and worship God, declaring, "God is truly here among you."

Paul had said that tongues were a sign to unbelievers. Here he explained what it would seem like to interested unbelievers who came into a church that was speaking in tongues. What such a person needed was the prophesying, or giving out the truth of God. They needed to hear the gospel in a language they could understand.

REFLECT

Hopefully you are being helped in understanding what the apostle Paul wrote. Make a list of some important truths you have learned.

RESPOND

Talk with a friend about what you can do in communicating the gospel in an understandable language to another person. It is regretful if those who know the language of others do not share the message of eternal life.

RECEIVE

1 Corinthians 14:26

²⁶ Well, my brothers and sisters, let's summarize. When you meet together, one will sing, another will teach, another will tell some special revelation God has given, one will speak in tongues, and another will interpret what is said. But everything that is done must strengthen all of you.

Paul gave a summary of what he had been writing. He mentioned those who sing; those who teach; those who have a special revelation from God; those who speak in tongues; and those who interpret what was said in the tongues. His bottom line was that "everything that is done must strengthen all of you." This meant all had to be done to build up the entire church group.

REFLECT

How is it done in your church group? Is everything done to strengthen the entire group?

RESPOND

Visit with a fellow church member to talk about the service in your church. Are things done to help everyone grow stronger in the Lord? What would you suggest to the leadership if you were asked?

WEEK 33:
1 CORINTHIANS 14

RECEIVE

1 Corinthians 14:27-28

27 No more than two or three should speak in tongues. They must speak one at a time, and someone must interpret what they say. 28 But if no one is present who can interpret, they must be silent in your church meeting and speak in tongues to God privately.

Paul laid down rules that were to be followed both in New Testament times and by any church who practices these gifts today. He gave a limit on how many tongues-speakers are allowed to speak. They are not to speak at all if there is no one there to interpret the languages they are speaking. If no interpreter is present, they can speak only to God but not to the church congregation.

REFLECT

Are you aware of churches today that are not following these rules? If so, they are not following God's inspired word.

RESPOND

Visit with a friend about friends or churches you know who practice tongues speaking. Do they follow the apostle Paul's rules?

RECEIVE

1 Corinthians 14:29-31

²⁹ Let two or three people prophesy, and let the others evaluate what is said. ³⁰ But if someone is prophesying and another person receives a revelation from the Lord, the one who is speaking must stop. ³¹ In this way, all who prophesy will have a turn to speak, one after the other, so that everyone will learn and be encouraged.

What was true of the tongues speakers was also to be true of those who had the gift of prophecy. Notice that there were not to be two people speaking at the same time. If a second person received a revelation and began speaking, the first speaker was to stop. The purpose of doing things this way was "so that everyone will learn and be encouraged." The whole group needed to be edified.

REFLECT

Are you impressed with how many times Paul said that what was done should be for the benefit of the entire group?

RESPOND

Leaders in churches today should still follow Paul's injunction given in Ephesians 4:12. Discuss this verse with a friend.

RECEIVE

DAY 3

1 Corinthians 14:32–33

[32] Remember that people who prophesy are in control of their spirit and can take turns. [33] For God is not a God of disorder but of peace, as in all the meetings of God's holy people.

Occasionally there could be the person who claims to have a revelation from God and insists on speaking even if someone else is. Paul wrote that the gifted person is to be in control of his gift. If two or more people speak at the same time that would cause disorder and no one would understand what is being said. Paul says that would not be coming from God because He is the God of peace.

REFLECT

Have you noticed when listening to radio or television that when more than one person speaks at the same time you cannot understand either one? Paul wanted that to be avoided in the church.

RESPOND

Visit with a friend about proper manners that should be taught in the home and practiced when in public. This would especially have to do with interrupting others. Paul also wanted proper manners to be followed in the church assembly.

RECEIVE

1 Corinthians 14:34-35

[34] Women should be silent during the church meetings. It is not proper for them to speak. They should be submissive, just as the law says. [35] If they have any questions, they should ask their husbands at home, for it is improper for women to speak in church meetings.

There are various interpretations of Paul's comment that women "should be silent during the church meetings." Inasmuch as he referred to asking husbands at home, the topic at least refers to married women whose husbands are in the service. Women had been known to speak. Philip had four daughters who had the gift of prophecy (see Acts 21:8-9). Remember the topic about speaking in 1 Corinthians 14 has to do with speaking in tongues, and that may be what Paul was referring to here.

REFLECT

Husbands are intended to take a leadership role in their homes as well as in churches. Regrettably, many wives have to attend church without their husbands.

RESPOND

The instructions Paul gave about husbands and wives in Ephesians 5:21-33 refer to a marriage of Christians. These comments have to do with an ideal relationship for them, but are not workable with unbelievers.

RECEIVE

1 Corinthians 14:36-38

[36] Or do you think God's word originated with you Corinthians? Are you the only ones to whom it was given? [37] If you claim to be a prophet or think you are spiritual, you should recognize that what I am saying is a command from the Lord himself. [38] But if you do not recognize this, you yourself will not be recognized.

What Paul had been expressing was considered common practice among the churches. If the Corinthians were of a different opinion they were acting as if only they had God's word on the subject. As an apostle, Paul had instructed what he had received from the Lord. It was not up to the local church in Corinth to decide what they thought was the right thing to do.

REFLECT

Does this help you to see that the basic question believers need to answer is, "Is the Bible the final authority on what we believe?" This means it is superior to what any denomination or church teaches.

RESPOND

Visit with a friend about some of the differences various church groups and denominations have. Does what they teach come from the Bible or from denominational beliefs? It is good to remember that in the first century there were no clergy/laity divisions as seen today, nor were there any denominations. Believers just told others what the apostles had taught. Those who became believers had the passion to share their faith with others and that spread the gospel to the then-known world.

WEEK 34:
1 CORINTHIANS 14, 15

RECEIVE

1 Corinthians 14:39-40

³⁹ So, my dear brothers and sisters, be eager to prophesy, and don't forbid speaking in tongues. ⁴⁰ But be sure that everything is done properly and in order.

Paul wanted the Corinthian believers to be "eager to prophesy." This gift would not need interpretation. He also said, "don't forbid speaking in tongues." This statement is claimed by some to think that should still be said today. The apostle Paul, however, never referred to speaking in tongues except when he was seeking to solve problems in Corinth. The completed Bible is available today and there is no need for further revelation (see Jude 1:3).

REFLECT

Does it not seem important and significant that Paul never referred to speaking in tongues except when he was trying to correct the problem in the Corinthian church about A.D. 55?

RESPOND

Visit with a friend about what Paul said in 1 Corinthians 14:40. He was concerned that "everything is done properly and in order." Is this the way things are done in your church?

DAY 2

RECEIVE

1 Corinthians 15:1–2

¹ Let me now remind you, dear brothers and sisters, of the Good News I preached to you before. You welcomed it then, and you still stand firm in it. ² It is this Good News that saves you if you continue to believe the message I told you—unless, of course, you believed something that was never true in the first place.

The "Good News" is a translation of the Greek word also translated "gospel." Paul wanted to remind them of what he had told them previously. Belief in the gospel he is about to remind them of is what saved them, he said. That is, of course, unless they had believed something that was never true in the first place. He was concerned about whether they had really believed the gospel or had some notion about how to get right with God apart from believing the gospel.

REFLECT

What would your answer be if you were asked, "What do you mean by the word 'gospel'?"

RESPOND

Talk with a friend about knowing certain titles for chapters in the Bible. For example, 1 Corinthians 13 is known as the love chapter. Hebrews 11 is known as the faith chapter. As you study 1 Corinthians 15, you will find it easy to come up with a name for it.

RECEIVE

DAY 3

1 Corinthians 15:3-4

³ I passed on to you what was most important and what had also been passed on to me. Christ died for our sins, just as the Scriptures said. ⁴ He was buried, and he was raised from the dead on the third day, just as the Scriptures said.

Paul reminded the Corinthian church of what he had taught them. Consider the items he mentioned here: 1) Christ died for our sins; 2) He was buried; 3) and He was raised from the dead on the third day. Paul emphasized his teaching was "as the Scriptures said." He likely here referred to revelation he received from Jesus after his conversion.

REFLECT

In searching online about a church group, be sure to notice whether they believe in the death, burial and resurrection of the Lord Jesus Christ.

RESPOND

There are many who believe Jesus died and was buried. There are fewer who believe He rose bodily from the grave. Some who even stand behind pulpits do not teach the bodily resurrection of the Lord Jesus. 1 Corinthians 15, which might be called the resurrection chapter, will show there is no hope for salvation unless you believe in the risen Christ. Of all the religious leaders in the past, only the grave of the Lord Jesus is empty.

RECEIVE

DAY 4

1 Corinthians 15:5-7

[5] He was seen by Peter and then by the Twelve. [6] After that, he was seen by more than 500 of his followers at one time, most of whom are still alive, though some have died. [7] Then he was seen by James and later by all the apostles.

In the Greek New Testament there is a small word *hoti* that appears before each item in the gospel message. This is not seen in English. The gospel is *that* Jesus died, *that* He was buried, and *that* He rose from the dead. There is a fourth *that* when Paul writes *that* He was seen by witnesses that he enumerates. Without witnesses there would have been no proof of Jesus' resurrection.

REFLECT

Think of this: over 500 at one time saw Jesus after His resurrection! No one can deny eyewitnesses.

RESPOND

Talk with a friend about Paul's comment that of those 500 who saw Jesus at one time, "most of whom are still alive." That was as if Paul were saying, "You don't have to believe me, go ask them."

RECEIVE

1 Corinthians 15:8–9

⁸ Last of all, as though I had been born at the wrong time, I also saw him. ⁹ For I am the least of all the apostles. In fact, I'm not even worthy to be called an apostle after the way I persecuted God's church.

Paul referred to Jesus appearing to him as if he had been born at the wrong time. This causes some to think that Paul should have been chosen as the 12ᵗʰ disciple after Judas defected. Acts 1:21-22, however, reveals the qualifications that Paul could not have met. His expression "born at the wrong time" does not indicate a late birth but an early birth. He likely saw himself as a Jew born before the national conversion of Israel.

REFLECT

Do you feel unworthy of what Jesus has done for you? So did Paul. No one is worthy; it is all of God's grace that anyone is saved.

RESPOND

See Acts 8:1-3 to see what occurred after Stephen was stoned to death for his faith. Saul was watching his accusers' clothes. "Saul" was his Hebrew name; "Paul" was his Gentile or Roman name. When God later sent him to the Gentiles he went by his Gentile name. It was common in a multilingual culture to have more than one name. Jesus' Hebrew name was *Yeshua*; His Greek name was *Iēsous*.

WEEK 35:
1 CORINTHIANS 15

RECEIVE

1 Corinthians 15:10-11

[10] But whatever I am now, it is all because God poured out his special favor on me—and not without results. For I have worked harder than any of the other apostles; yet it was not I but God who was working through me by his grace. [11] So it makes no difference whether I preach or they preach, for we all preach the same message you have already believed.

Paul felt unworthy but he thanked God for His grace apart from any of Paul's good works. Beyond his salvation, Paul realized that God had continued to work through him as he preached the gospel to others. Paul did not set himself up as the best example. Whether he preached or the others preached, it was the same message that had been preached to the Corinthians.

REFLECT

As a believer in Jesus, do you realize you are part of a group speaking the same message to others if they teach the Bible and the Bible alone? The particular messenger is not as important as the message.

RESPOND

The Corinthians were divided about who was the better preacher: Paul or Apollos. Read 1 Corinthians 3:3-5 to see Paul saw this as living an unspiritual life. Discuss with a friend how this might apply to you today as you talk about who is the better pastor.

RECEIVE

1 Corinthians 15:12-15

[12] But tell me this—since we preach that Christ rose from the dead, why are some of you saying there will be no resurrection of the dead? [13] For if there is no resurrection of the dead, then Christ has not been raised either. [14] And if Christ has not been raised, then all our preaching is useless, and your faith is useless. [15] And we apostles would all be lying about God—for we have said that God raised Christ from the grave. But that can't be true if there is no resurrection of the dead.

At the time Paul was writing this, there were those who did not believe in the physical resurrection of the body. Paul stressed if they really believed there was no resurrection of the dead, then they also must believe that Christ had not risen from the dead. He enumerated some of the extreme consequences of not believing Christ had risen from the dead. Even their faith would be useless if that were not true.

REFLECT

What do you believe about this key belief? Did Christ bodily rise from the dead or not? Your salvation depends on what you believe.

RESPOND

Join with a friend in reading Acts 1:3. There you will see that faith in the resurrected Christ is not a "leap in the dark" but faith based on the facts.

RECEIVE

DAY 3

1 Corinthians 15:16-20

[16] And if there is no resurrection of the dead, then Christ has not been raised. [17] And if Christ has not been raised, then your faith is useless and you are still guilty of your sins. [18] In that case, all who have died believing in Christ are lost! [19] And if our hope in Christ is only for this life, we are more to be pitied than anyone in the world. [20] But in fact, Christ has been raised from the dead. He is the first of a great harvest of all who have died.

Paul told the Corinthians that if Christ had not been raised from the dead they were still guilty of their sins. Plus, all their loved ones who had died believing in Jesus are actually lost. The apostle insisted that Christ had been raised from the dead and is the first in line of a great harvest of those who have died.

REFLECT

Because Jesus has risen from the dead you can count on what He said in John 11:25.

RESPOND

Almost everyone is concerned about the eternal destiny of their loved ones who have passed away. For those who have placed faith in Jesus, we can be assured that to be absent from the body is to be present with the Lord (see 2 Corinthians 5:8).

RECEIVE

DAY 4

1 Corinthians 15:21–23

²¹ So you see, just as death came into the world through a man, now the resurrection from the dead has begun through another man. ²² Just as everyone dies because we all belong to Adam, everyone who belongs to Christ will be given new life. ²³ But there is an order to this resurrection: Christ was raised as the first of the harvest; then all who belong to Christ will be raised when he comes back.

Paul compared Adam and Christ. Because Adam disobeyed God, his sin poisoned all of his descendants so each of them has been born in sin (see Romans 5:12). Because of this, all are condemned (see John 3:18). In contrast to Adam, Christ brought eternal life to all who believe in Him. Paul referred to Jesus and His resurrection as being "the first of the harvest." Later, others who believe in Him will be raised from the dead.

REFLECT

Rejoice that if you believe in Jesus you will have eternal life as promised in John 3:16.

RESPOND

With a friend read Romans 5:20–21. This passage contrasts death that came from God's law and eternal life that comes through the grace of God.

DAY 5

RECEIVE

1 Corinthians 15:24-26

²⁴ After that the end will come, when he will turn the Kingdom over to God the Father, having destroyed every ruler and authority and power. ²⁵ For Christ must reign until he humbles all his enemies beneath his feet. ²⁶ And the last enemy to be destroyed is death.

In considering the order of the resurrections, Paul lists Christ as the first fruits (an evidence of more to come), and all who are His when He returns. In 1 Corinthians 15:24, Paul mentioned Jesus turning over everything to the Father after He has "destroyed every ruler and authority and power." The last enemy to be conquered is death. Physical death comes to all except believers caught up at the rapture (see 1 Thessalonians 4:13-18). All other believers will die, but they can rest in the promise of Jesus as recorded in John 11:25.

REFLECT

Death is an ugly thing that God never intended to occur to mankind. It is because of Adam's sin that it has affected the human race. But beyond death for the believer is eternity with Jesus.

RESPOND

Join with a Christian friend in reading Romans 8:18-25. Rejoice together in the future hope you have.

WEEK 36:
1 CORINTHIANS 15

RECEIVE

1 Corinthians 15:27

²⁷ For the Scriptures say, "God has put all things under his authority." (Of course, when it says "all things are under his authority," that does not include God himself, who gave Christ his authority.)

After saying that Jesus will destroy death as the last enemy, Paul writes about who will not be put under His authority. In 1 Corinthians 11:3 Paul tells how there is ranking in the Godhead. From this it is learned that Jesus is the Second Person of the Trinity. He is in submission to the heavenly Father.

REFLECT

Do you realize there is even submission among the Godhead of Father, Son and Holy Spirit?

RESPOND

With a friend read John 1:1-3 to see that the Father created everything by means of or through Jesus. See also Colossians 1:15-16 in this regard.

RECEIVE

1 Corinthians 15:28

²⁸ Then, when all things are under his authority, the Son will put himself under God's authority, so that God, who gave his Son authority over all things, will be utterly supreme over everything everywhere.

After Jesus has put all things under His authority, He will submit Himself to the heavenly Father. The Father had given the Son all authority; finally the Son will return all authority to the Father. This will make the Father "supreme over everything everywhere."

REFLECT

As a believer in Jesus, do you realize you serve a sovereign God because He is supreme over everything?

RESPOND

Even in the Old Testament it is seen that the psalmist realized God was supreme. Read Psalm 97:8-9 as an example.

RECEIVE

1 Corinthians 15:29

²⁹ If the dead will not be raised, what point is there in people being baptized for those who are dead? Why do it unless the dead will someday rise again?

This verse has many different interpretations. A counterfeit religious group even uses it to suggest you should get baptized for a person who has died. This would make the person you were baptized for a follower of their religion. No other Scripture supports such a view. It is far better to understand the verse as referring to new believers taking the place of other believers who have passed away.

REFLECT

As a believer in Jesus, you can consider yourself as taking the place of another believer who has passed away.

RESPOND

In some parts of the world believers have died because of proclaiming their belief in Jesus. You now can help take their place by being a faithful witness yourself. This is a reminder that there are many people in heaven now who have given their lives for the sake of the gospel.

RECEIVE

DAY 4

1 Corinthians 15:30-31

³⁰ And why should we ourselves risk our lives hour by hour? ³¹ For I swear, dear brothers and sisters, that I face death daily. This is as certain as my pride in what Christ Jesus our Lord has done in you.

Remember that Paul was writing about the resurrection and proving its validity. He asks why he and others should risk their lives in proclaiming the gospel if there is no resurrection. Some translations render verse 31 as, "I die daily." There are those who take this in a spiritual sense. In the context, Paul was referring to risking his physical life every day.

REFLECT

Are you thankful for others who have risked their lives to tell people about Jesus? Some are still doing this today.

RESPOND

Join with a friend in praying for those today who are risking their lives to tell others about Jesus. If you can tell others about Jesus without risking your life, are you doing it?

RECEIVE

1 Corinthians 15:32

³² And what value was there in fighting wild beasts—those people of Ephesus—if there will be no resurrection from the dead? And if there is no resurrection, "Let's feast and drink, for tomorrow we die!"

Paul likened the unbelievers of Ephesus to be like fighting with wild beasts. He realized he could lose his life at any time. The reason Paul considered all of this to be worthwhile was because he believed in a physical resurrection. For those who really think there is no resurrection, they may as well feast and drink now because death is the end for them. Not for Paul who believed in the resurrection.

REFLECT

Do you have some verses in the Bible to turn to as you think about death? If not, begin to search for some.

RESPOND

Talk with a friend about what Bible verses could be used to comfort the grieving at the time of death of a believing loved one. Consider such as these: Psalm 17:15; 34:18; 116:15; Isaiah 43:2; John 11:25. It can also be helpful to copy out a reference in a sympathy card.

WEEK 37:
1 CORINTHIANS 15

RECEIVE

1 Corinthians 15:33-34

[33] Don't be fooled by those who say such things, for "bad company corrupts good character." [34] Think carefully about what is right, and stop sinning. For to your shame I say that some of you don't know God at all.

This was Paul's answer to some who thought there is no resurrection so you might as well eat and drink because tomorrow you die. Paul was direct when he wrote that "some of you don't know God at all." Those who deny the resurrection of Jesus have no salvation.

REFLECT

Does this help you to see how serious it is to deny the resurrection of Jesus?

RESPOND

It is one thing to talk about the life and death of Jesus, but notice what occurs when you talk about His resurrection. This happened to Paul when he was addressing the idol worshipers in Athens (see Acts 17:16-34).

RECEIVE

1 Corinthians 15:35-37

[35] But someone may ask, "How will the dead be raised? What kind of bodies will they have?" [36] What a foolish question! When you put a seed into the ground, it doesn't grow into a plant unless it dies first. [37] And what you put in the ground is not the plant that will grow, but only a bare seed of wheat or whatever you are planting.

Paul used an example from their agricultural life to explain about a change at the resurrection. For the seed to grow it had to die first. Before bodies will be resurrected they must die first. Paul was providing hope that looked beyond the grave.

REFLECT

You may have questions about how things will work out in eternity. For believers it will be a perfect place and you can trust Jesus for everything.

RESPOND

Visit with a friend about having confidence in what Jesus said. His comments about believers being with Him are seen in John 14:1-3; 11:25; Romans 6:7-9.

RECEIVE

DAY 3

1 Corinthians 15:38-39

[38] Then God gives it the new body he wants it to have. A different plant grows from each kind of seed. [39] Similarly there are different kinds of flesh—one kind for humans, another for animals, another for birds, and another for fish.

After the body dies, like grain that dies and then produces fruit, God gives a new body. Paul did not believe in evolution; he listed the different kinds of flesh for humans, animals, birds and fish. The Genesis account reveals God's design was for His created life to reproduce "after their kind" (see Genesis 1:11-12, 21, 24-25). God also created man "in his own image" (Genesis 1:26-27).

REFLECT

Do you realize that one "kind" never becomes another "kind" even though there are various species in each kind?

RESPOND

Whether one believes in evolution or creation it must be taken by faith because no human was there to witness it. With a friend, read Hebrews 11:3 as a reminder.

RECEIVE

1 Corinthians 15:40-41

⁴⁰ There are also bodies in the heavens and bodies on the earth. The glory of the heavenly bodies is different from the glory of the earthly bodies. ⁴¹ The sun has one kind of glory, while the moon and stars each have another kind. And even the stars differ from each other in their glory.

Paul continued to contrast earthly bodies with heavenly ones. Remember that he was writing to prove his point about the resurrection of the physical body. There were those in his day who were teaching that only spirit is good and material is bad so there would be no resurrection of the body. A group doing this was known as the "Gnostics." This word had to do with knowledge, and Paul was demonstrating that their so-called knowledge was wrong.

REFLECT

Brilliant people are as lost as ignorant unbelievers if they don't have faith in Jesus.

RESPOND

Join with a friend in reading 1 Corinthians 2:12-16. This will remind you that the unsaved (natural) person does not understand the things of God.

DAY 5

RECEIVE

1 Corinthians 15:42–44

[42] It is the same way with the resurrection of the dead. Our earthly bodies are planted in the ground when we die, but they will be raised to live forever. [43] Our bodies are buried in brokenness, but they will be raised in glory. They are buried in weakness, but they will be raised in strength. [44] They are buried as natural human bodies, but they will be raised as spiritual bodies. For just as there are natural bodies, there are also spiritual bodies.

Paul here contrasted what it will be like when the believer's body is resurrected from the grave. Here on earth even Christ followers have bodies of weakness and pain. Someday, however, they will be given glorified bodies that will never experience pain. All the former things will pass away and "there will be no more death or sorrow or crying or pain. All these things are gone forever" (Revelation 21:4).

REFLECT

As a believer, no matter what you are experiencing now, think of how wonderful it will be for you in the future.

RESPOND

Join with a friend in reading John 12:25–26. This passage records the words of Jesus about people who value this life more than the life hereafter. It is also an appeal for believers to serve the Lord Jesus.

WEEK 38:
1 CORINTHIANS 15

RECEIVE

1 Corinthians 15:45-47

45 The Scriptures tell us, "The first man, Adam, became a living person." But the last Adam—that is, Christ—is a life-giving Spirit. 46 What comes first is the natural body, then the spiritual body comes later. 47 Adam, the first man, was made from the dust of the earth, while Christ, the second man, came from heaven.

Paul contrasted the first and last Adams. The one created in Genesis 2:7 was a person made from the dust on the earth. The first Adam who came from dust disobeyed God and poisoned the human race with a fallen sin nature. The last Adam—that is, Christ, has always existed and came from heaven, was born as a baby and grew to manhood to give His life for the sins of the world. Christ gives eternal life to all who believe in Him.

REFLECT

Notice how the apostle Paul kept referring to the Scriptures. That is what every believer should do when faced with a spiritual question.

RESPOND

With a friend read Acts 17:10-12. Some people even change churches so they can go to where the Scriptures are taught. How is it in your church fellowship? Are the Scriptures taught and explained? See Nehemiah 8:8 for how it was done in Old Testament times.

DAY 2

RECEIVE

1 Corinthians 15:48-49

⁴⁸ Earthly people are like the earthly man, and heavenly people are like the heavenly man. ⁴⁹ Just as we are now like the earthly man, we will someday be like the heavenly man.

Paul contrasted the earthly person with the heavenly person. Those alive now are like the earthly person. Someday believers in Jesus will be like the heavenly person when they are taken to heaven in their changed bodies.

REFLECT

As a believer do you look forward to receiving your heavenly body that will be without pain or suffering and will never know death?

RESPOND

Join with your friend in reading 1 Thessalonians 4:13-18. This tells of the time when believers will be caught up to meet Jesus in the air. Those believers who have already passed away will rise first followed by believers living at that time.

RECEIVE

DAY 3

1 Corinthians 15:50

⁵⁰ What I am saying, dear brothers and sisters, is that our physical bodies cannot inherit the Kingdom of God. These dying bodies cannot inherit what will last forever.

Just as planted grain could not be transformed until it died, so also the physical body will not inherit God's Kingdom. Believers will receive a body that "will last forever." That is the inheritance to which every believer can look forward.

REFLECT

Christ followers can rejoice as they think about the time when they will receive heavenly bodies that will last forever.

RESPOND

Together with a friend read what Paul said in his second letter to the Corinthians. In 2 Corinthians 4:16-18 he contrasted the present problems with the future.

RECEIVE

1 Corinthians 15:51–52

[51] But let me reveal to you a wonderful secret. We will not all die, but we will all be transformed! [52] It will happen in a moment, in the blink of an eye, when the last trumpet is blown. For when the trumpet sounds, those who have died will be raised to live forever. And we who are living will also be transformed.

Paul referred to a "secret" in that it had not been revealed in the Old Testament. It was that believers will be changed from their earthly bodies to their heavenly bodies in the blink of an eye. Those raised from the dead and transformed will live forever.

REFLECT

Think often about this wonderful truth.

RESPOND

Seek to minister to others who have had believing loved ones pass away. Remind them that someday those believers will be transformed into their heavenly bodies.

DAY 5

RECEIVE

1 Corinthians 15:53

⁵³ For our dying bodies must be transformed into bodies that will never die; our mortal bodies must be transformed into immortal bodies.

Paul continued his thoughts about mortal believers who die and are transformed into their immortal bodies. This is the way earthly bodies take on heavenly bodies. Paul had been writing these truths to encourage the believers in Corinth to realize there will be a resurrection of the body, just as Jesus' body was resurrected from the grave.

REFLECT

To be "transformed" is to have the form changed. This will be that wonderful time when believers have the form of their earthly bodies changed into the form of their heavenly bodies.

RESPOND

Paul also wrote about something believers can do to have their forms changed while here on earth. See Romans 12:1-2 in this regard. Notice that verse 2 in this passage focuses on changing the way one thinks. A believer can be a witness by his life, language and thought life.

WEEK 39:
1 CORINTHIANS 15, 16

RECEIVE

1 Corinthians 15:54-55

54 Then, when our dying bodies have been transformed into bodies that will never die, this Scripture will be fulfilled: "Death is swallowed up in victory. 55 O death, where is your victory? O death, where is your sting?"

The apostle Paul assured believers in Jesus that when their bodies are transformed, death will be swallowed up in victory. Usually death is thought of as the greatest defeat of all but not for the believer. It even removes the sting of death for the believer.

REFLECT

As a believer in Jesus, do you think differently about physical death than before you became a believer?

RESPOND

Talk with a believer about these verses. No one likes to think about death and leaving loved ones behind. But it is a glorious thought that the last breath on earth is the first one in heaven. Read 2 Corinthians 5:6-8 in this regard.

RECEIVE

DAY 2

1 Corinthians 15:56-57

56 For sin is the sting that results in death, and the law gives sin its power. 57 But thank God! He gives us victory over sin and death through our Lord Jesus Christ.

Paul told what the sting of death is. It is sin that results in death. This refers to the inherited sin nature, not necessarily acts of sin. Paul praised God in spite of this when he exclaimed, "But thank God!" Because of what Jesus Christ accomplished for believers in Him, they have "victory over sin and death."

REFLECT

Does what Paul wrote enable you to praise God for what has been accomplished for you through Jesus Christ?

RESPOND

Join with a friend to talk about what has occurred to the human race since Adam disobeyed God. Adam's sin poisoned all his descendants and caused them to be born in sin. Romans 5:12 tells about death resulting from this inherited sin nature.

RECEIVE

DAY 3

1 Corinthians 15:58

⁵⁸ So, my dear brothers and sisters, be strong and immovable. Always work enthusiastically for the Lord, for you know that nothing you do for the Lord is ever useless.

What he was writing caused the apostle Paul to urge believers to be "strong and immovable." Rather than regretting how each day is going, he wanted Christians to always "work enthusiastically for the Lord." Some consider their tasks to be mundane and unspiritual, but Paul told them "nothing you do for the Lord is ever useless." Work with the Lord in view.

REFLECT

Think of the things you've done over the last few days. Consider them all to have been useful as long as you were doing them to honor the Lord.

RESPOND

As you think about honoring Jesus with all you do, read Colossians 3:17. Make this a key verse in your life.

RECEIVE

DAY 4

1 Corinthians 16:1-2

[1] Now regarding your question about the money being collected for God's people in Jerusalem. You should follow the same procedure I gave to the churches in Galatia. [2] On the first day of each week, you should each put aside a portion of the money you have earned. Don't wait until I get there and then try to collect it all at once.

Paul dealt with the questions the Corinthians had asked him. He had taken up offerings to help the persecuted Jews in Jerusalem. Apparently the Corinthians wondered how to handle this. Paul gave the principle for New Testament giving in verse 2. Notice he did not refer to a tithe. The tithe is mentioned in the New Testament only in referring to the practice in the Old Testament. Paul's comment is considered "proportional giving"—as you have been blessed.

REFLECT

What do you use as a guide in your giving?

RESPOND

See what Paul later wrote to the Corinthians in 2 Corinthians 8:10-15. Note the various principles he stated in these verses. Discuss them with a friend.

RECEIVE

DAY 5

1 Corinthians 16:3-4

³ When I come, I will write letters of recommendation for the messengers you choose to deliver your gift to Jerusalem. ⁴ And if it seems appropriate for me to go along, they can travel with me.

Notice how careful Paul was about the way money should be handled. It would not be sent with only a single messenger. He would even allow the Corinthians to choose the messengers. Plus, even he might go with them. Too often money is handled by only one person. If he or she is falsely charged about something, how would the person be cleared of any guilt?

REFLECT

Do you realize the need to be extra careful in handling money for others?

RESPOND

The love of money has caused many to dishonor the Lord by taking what is not theirs. See 1 Timothy 6:9-10 and guard against problems. See also Matthew 6:24.

WEEK 40:
1 CORINTHIANS 16

RECEIVE

1 Corinthians 16:5-6

[5] I am coming to visit you after I have been to Macedonia, for I am planning to travel through Macedonia. [6] Perhaps I will stay awhile with you, possibly all winter, and then you can send me on my way to my next destination.

It must have been encouraging for the Corinthians to read that Paul planned to visit them. Macedonia was in the north and then he would come to the south to visit the believers in Corinth. He did not plan just a short visit and thought he might stay with them all winter. Think how much they would have learned from the apostle if he stayed that long.

REFLECT

Consider how wonderful it would be to spend a few months with the apostle Paul.

RESPOND

Talk with a friend about what it might have been like to spend time with an apostle or even Jesus Himself. Remind yourselves that there is even a greater privilege today because God's completed revelation is available in the Bible. Believers also have the Holy Spirit living in them to teach them the Bible. See John 16:7-15 to see what Jesus said before His ascension to heaven.

RECEIVE

1 Corinthians 16:7-9

⁷ This time I don't want to make just a short visit and then go right on. I want to come and stay awhile, if the Lord will let me. ⁸ In the meantime, I will be staying here at Ephesus until the Festival of Pentecost. ⁹ There is a wide-open door for a great work here, although many oppose me.

Paul again expressed his desire to stay with the Corinthians for a long visit. Verse 8 in this passage is the one that says the place from which Paul was writing 1 Corinthians to them. The Festival of Pentecost was an annual celebration even from Old Testament times. Paul had an open door of ministry in Ephesus, but he also had many adversaries.

REFLECT

Have you noticed when you have opportunities to witness there is also some opposition?

RESPOND

Join with a friend to talk about opposition and blessing in ministry. Read 2 Corinthians 4:3-4 and Ephesians 6:10-12 to see why you have opposition.

RECEIVE

DAY 3

1 Corinthians 16:10–11

¹⁰ When Timothy comes, don't intimidate him. He is doing the Lord's work, just as I am. ¹¹ Don't let anyone treat him with contempt. Send him on his way with your blessing when he returns to me. I expect him to come with the other believers.

Timothy was a dear companion of the apostle Paul. He wanted the Corinthians to treat him with great respect. Paul looked forward to seeing Timothy again when he came with other believers. Paul's affection and discipling of Timothy causes some Christian leaders to say, "Everyone needs a Paul, and every Paul needs a Timothy."

REFLECT

Do you have a close companion in ministry as Paul had with Timothy? Ask God to give you one.

RESPOND

Read about Timothy in various Scripture passages. See Acts 16:1–3 for when Paul first met him. Read Romans 16:21; 2 Corinthians 1:1; Philippians 1:1; 2:20–22; Colossians 1:1; 1 Thessalonians 1:1; Philemon 1:1 to see Timothy was often addressed in letters along with Paul. See 1 Timothy 1:1–3 and 2 Timothy 1:1–3 to read how Paul addressed Timothy in his personal letters to him.

RECEIVE

1 Corinthians 16:12

[12] Now about our brother Apollos—I urged him to visit you with the other believers, but he was not willing to go right now. He will see you later when he has the opportunity.

Remember, in 1 Corinthians 1:12 Paul wrote that the Corinthians were divided about whom they should follow. Apollos is mentioned there but in 1 Corinthians 16:12, as well as in other places, Paul reveals there was no competition between them because he was glad to recommend him to others.

REFLECT

Have you noticed that sometimes people think there are more differences between Christian leaders than there really are?

RESPOND

Join with a friend in reading further about what Paul said about Apollos. Read 1 Corinthians 3:1-9 to notice how both Paul and Apollos were doing the Lord's work. As you plant spiritual seed in the lives of others with your Christian witness, pray others will come along later and water and some will be able to pick the spiritual fruit.

RECEIVE

1 Corinthians 16:13-14

¹³ Be on guard. Stand firm in the faith. Be courageous. Be strong.
¹⁴ And do everything with love.

Paul continued his concluding remarks to the Corinthians by urging them with four commands. Notice he added a fifth command that they should "do everything with love." They had been guilty of not showing love at the Lord's Table and with exercising spiritual gifts. That's why he wrote what he did in 1 Corinthians 13.

REFLECT

Have you noticed that some who emphasize truth do not speak it with love?

RESPOND

Visit with a friend about how important it is to love the truth, but to speak the truth in love. Review your past week and ask how you could have done it better.

WEEK 41:
1 CORINTHIANS 16

RECEIVE

1 Corinthians 16:15-16

[15] You know that Stephanas and his household were the first of the harvest of believers in Greece, and they are spending their lives in service to God's people. I urge you, dear brothers and sisters, [16] to submit to them and others like them who serve with such devotion.

Paul had good memories of those who trusted Jesus early in his ministry in Greece. They had not only trusted in Jesus as Savior but spent their lives in service to God's people. Paul wanted the Corinthians to submit to those who were serving with such devotion.

REFLECT

Have you watched others who are fervently serving the Lord and desire to model your life after them?

RESPOND

Join with a friend in reading Philippians 3:17. Talk about more mature believers you might pattern your life after.

RECEIVE

DAY 2

1 Corinthians 16:17-18

[17] I am very glad that Stephanas, Fortunatus, and Achaicus have come here. They have been providing the help you weren't here to give me. [18] They have been a wonderful encouragement to me, as they have been to you. You must show your appreciation to all who serve so well.

Paul had mentioned Stephanas before, but there are no other references to Fortunatus and Achaicus in the New Testament. These last two might be unknown to today's readers, but Paul knew them as wonderful encouragers. He wanted the Corinthians to be appreciative of them.

REFLECT

Do you know of some who are outstanding in encouraging others? The world may not know about them, but you can express your appreciation for them.

RESPOND

Talk with a friend about Christians who are an example to you. Thank them for the spiritual ministry they have and make it your desire to be like them.

RECEIVE

1 Corinthians 16:19–20

[19] The churches here in the province of Asia send greetings in the Lord, as do Aquila and Priscilla and all the others who gather in their home for church meetings. [20] All the brothers and sisters here send greetings to you. Greet each other with a sacred kiss.

Paul sent greetings from the churches in what is now known as Asia Minor. He added in his greetings to them from Aquila and Priscilla. Paul also included greetings from those who met in their home. He commanded the Corinthians to greet each other with a holy, or sacred, kiss.

REFLECT

Are you encouraged when you learn that greetings are being sent to you from other believers?

RESPOND

Talk with a believer about what the common manner is for your church group to greet each other. Judas had betrayed Jesus with a kiss. His was certainly not one of affection. Perhaps that is why Paul clarified what kind of kiss it should be.

RECEIVE

DAY 4

1 Corinthians 16:21

²¹ HERE IS MY GREETING IN MY OWN HANDWRITING—PAUL.

It was common for Paul to dictate a letter to a coworker. Here he took the pen in hand and wrote in large letters his name in his own handwriting that would identify him as the author of it. It had been known that others sometimes had written and claimed to be Paul. This would assure his readers of his genuine authorship.

REFLECT

Think of your own family recognizing your handwriting and knowing the letter is from you.

RESPOND

Look at some examples where Paul was aware others might write in his name. See 2 Thessalonians 2:1-4, and especially notice verse 2. See also Galatians 1:8-9 where he warned them that if they had seen anything from him or even an angel that was a different gospel, that person should be cursed. See also Galatians 6:11 where he signed with large letters.

RECEIVE

DAY 5

1 Corinthians 16:22-24

22 If anyone does not love the Lord, that person is cursed. Our Lord, come! 23 May the grace of the Lord Jesus be with you. 24 My love to all of you in Christ Jesus.

Paul closed his letter to the Corinthians with the somber warning that anyone who does not love the Lord is cursed. "Our Lord, come!" is from the Aramaic word *Maranatha.* He ended his letter with a reference to grace and love. As an unsaved Pharisee he marveled at the grace of God when he came to Christ in faith. He wanted the Corinthians to express love, and now he expressed his love to all of the believers.

REFLECT

Do you also reflect on the grace of God for your salvation? Do you express your love to other believers?

RESPOND

Talk with a believer about a strong Scripture passage about grace. See Ephesians 2:8-9. For the emphasis on love you could reread 1 Corinthians 13. Be thankful for what God has done in your life. Think also how you can express your love to other believers.

Personal Notes

This is the 11th book I have been pleased to publish on Amazon.com with the help of others. Those I wish to especially express appreciation for are Richard Sanne, editorial assistant; Renee Fisher, self-publishing expert; and Nelly Murariu, graphic designer.

The following is a list of the eleven books in the order they were published:

- *What They Believe: Studies of various religious groups*
- *Treasures from the Original, Vol. 1: 39 Greek Word Studies*
- *Treasures from the Original, Vol. 2: Studies in Philippians*
- *Treasures from the Original, Vol. 3: Studies in 2 Timothy*
- *John: An Eyewitness Report*
- *Genesis: Daily Scriptures to Receive, Reflect, and Respond*
- *Romans: Daily Scriptures to Receive, Reflect, and Respond*
- *Acts Volume 1: Daily Scriptures to Receive, Reflect, and Respond*
- *Acts Volume 2: Daily Scriptures to Receive, Reflect, and Respond*
- *Revelation: Daily Scriptures to Receive, Reflect, and Respond*
- *1 Corinthians: Daily Scriptures to Receive, Reflect and Respond*

My prayer is that God will use these volumes to reveal to readers how to become right with God and to live to glorify Him.

Harold J. Berry
ThM, DD
Lincoln, Nebraska

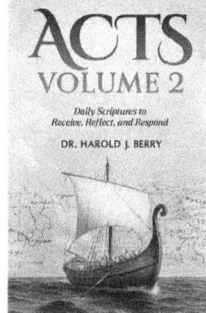

About the Author

Dr. Harold J. Berry is a former professor of Bible and Greek at Grace University of Omaha. He served for many years as personal assistant to Theodore H. Epp, founder of Back to the Bible. Dr. Berry holds a Master of Theology degree from Dallas Theological Seminary and a Doctor of Divinity from Grace University.

www.ingramcontent.com/pod-product-compliance
Lightning Source LLC
LaVergne TN
LVHW051359080426
835508LV00022B/2900